EXPLORING THE UPPER DEARNE VALLEY

ABOUT THE AUTHOR

JOHN WILKINSON was born in 1937 and has lived in West Bretton, within the Upper Dearne Valley, for most of his life. He was awarded the degree of Master of Arts in Theology at Birmingham University in 1964, and also holds the degree of Master of Arts of Leeds University in Education and Local History. From 1964 he was a schoolteacher and, in 1996, retired from the position of Head of Religious Studies in the school where he was a pupil – Queen Elizabeth Grammar School, Wakefield. He now works on a part-time basis as the School's archivist.

Married to Judith, also a retired schoolteacher, he has two sons – Andrew and Simon – who are pursuing careers in education and civil engineering respectively.

John has long been interested in local history. He has been collecting the material for this book for over ten years. In the course of his research he became so involved in the history of his own village that he delayed this publication in order to write *Farmstead of the Britons* – the historical story of West Bretton.

Exploration of record office, libraries and archives – together with old photograph albums and recorded oral memories – have led to a series of articles in various periodicals, to two BBC broadcasts – and now to this book.

Apart from the pursuit of local history, John is a very enthusiastic gardener. He is a Church of England Reader and an organist. Since 1986 he has been a magistrate in Wakefield and is currently the chairman of the Youth Panel.

John F. Wilkinson

Exploring THE UPPER DEARNE VALLEY

the LIFE and INDUSTRY
of a
YORKSHIRE PEOPLE

With a Foreword by
The Revd Baroness Richardson of Calow, O.B.E.

BRIDGE PUBLICATIONS
PENISTONE · ENGLAND

Bridge Publications
7 Rydal Close, Penistone
Sheffield S36 8HN

First Published 2002

A CIP catalogue record of this book is available from the British Library

ISBN 0-947934-34-0
ISBN 0-947934-33-2 (pbk)

Typeset in Times New Roman by Bridge Publications
Printed and Bound in Great Britain by
St Edmundsbury Press

For Judith
with gratitude for forty years of married life

Contents

Foreword

For some years I lived in the area which John Wilkinson describes so richly in this book. I have walked in its fields, picked its mushrooms, preached in its chapels, driven through its villages and eaten of its produce - particularly its harvest suppers. I have listened to its people with their opinions sharpened by rich traditions, different belief patterns, fiercely held views and (a few) prejudices.

What I find in this book stimulates my memories and gives substance to my impressions. I am amazed at the detail of its past and gladly recognise the variety of its present life. It also makes me want to return to walk there again with this book in my hands.

John writes for both residents and visitors, and I believe this book offers material that will enrich our experiences and help to encourage the conservation of a fascinating strand of English life. He is both observer and interpreter, but maybe more than this - a lover of this part of Yorkshire.

The Reverend Baroness Richardson of Calow, O.B.E.

Introduction

THE UPPER DEARNE VALLEY is not usually assessed as one of the classic Yorkshire dales, and its story is not one of the grand or spectacular. Little of its geographical features or economic and social life could be called 'large scale', yet careful exploration reveals a fascinating story which reflects so many of the isssues that have made England the nation that it is.

Neolithic settlement, medieval monastic industry and stately homes are all to be found here, but what we find especially is the story of the Industrial Revolution - clearly focusing our attention on workshops, mills, railways and the like, but also on changing beliefs and attitudes, as well as life-styles. Religious and political dissent exemplified in the rise of a once powerful Nonconformity, or sympathetic support of Luddism and Chartism are clear expressions of this.

Here we find also rich expressions of communal recreation - Emley Agricultural Show and the village's astonishingly successful football club, and the unique custom of baking enormous pies in Denby Dale.

This book does not attempt to present the full historical story of the valley. It is primarily concerned with features of local history which are still observable. The late Professor W.G. Hoskins who, according to the *Times Educational Supplement*, could read an English landscape as other people read a book, wrote:

> We live in a country that is richer than any other in the visible remains of the past ..... (but) ..... most of us are visually illiterate. The material evidence of the past is all around us, if only we can construe the language it is speaking .....

It has been my aim to present some of that 'material evidence'.

The book has been planned in such a way that it gives an overview of the various aspects of the valley's development followed by an account of each village. A map is included to facilitate a possible tour. Such an exploration may be followed from and to the M1 Motorway (Exit 38) in a matter of two or three hours or in two or three days - depending upon the depth to which the explorer wishes to go.

The responsibility for what has been written must be mine alone, but no historian works in a vacuum. Each village in the valley has its own historian and in reading what others have written I have enlarged my own vision and discovered pointers to a greater awareness. The sources that have been consulted are listed at the end.

My thanks go to many people who have generously given me help and advice. Mention must be made of staff at the Borthwick Institute of Historical Research in York, Bretton Hall University College, the Public Record Office in Kew, the libraries in Barnsley, Huddersfield and Wakefield, the Tolson Museum in Huddersfield, the West Yorkshire Archive Service and the Yorkshire Archeological Society.

I record my indebtedness to Mr & Mrs Stephen Brook of Wheatley Hill Farm for allowing me to take photographs both inside and outside their fascinating house; Kenneth Haigh of Denby Dale Parish Council for directing me towards several useful sources of information, and various people who have loaned or given me old photographs - especially the late Ted Banner, Lucie Froggatt, Geoffrey Sharp and Reg Stone. Staff at Nortonthorpe Mills provided information about and access to 'Violet' the steam engine; Tom Wood gave me some details about the Wesleyan Reform Church in Birdsedge; and Leslie Robinson and Stanley Sheead shared their expert knowledge of the textile industry in the area and a great deal about the history of Skelmanthorpe. My friend and former colleague, Paul Sutcliffe, very kindly designed the cover.

Acknowledgement is made of permission to use copyright material by:

The Rt Hon. the Viscount Allendale (the portrait of Sir Thomas Blackett by Thomas Gainsborough)

Nick Farman (the photograph of Cannon Hall at Cawthorne)

The Huddersfield District Chronicle (the programme for the Denby Dale Jubilee pie of 1896)

Kirklees Cultural Services (the photographs of an old coal mine at Denby Dale, Nortonthorpe Mill, the banner of the Skelmanthorpe Chartists, Cumberworth Road and The Green – Skelmanthorpe, High Bridge Road – Skelmanthorpe, and for allowing me to reproduce the photograph of the High Hoyland Cross in the Tolson Museum)

The family of the late Ronald Bielby (the photographs of the exterior and interior of Flockton United Reformed Church)

Chris Sharp (the photographs of Woolley Edge bonfire, the former Haigh Station and the former Haigh Methodist Chapel)

All other photographs are by the author, by Judith Wilkinson and by Edwin Parr.

Every attempt has been made to trace the owners of copyright. This has not been an easy task and, if any omissions are apparent, due acknowledgement will be made in any future edition.

Finally, I am indebted to Baroness Richardson of Calow (who may be described as an adopted daughter of the valley) for agreeing to write the foreword, and to Edwin Parr of Bridge Publications for agreeing to publish this work and for sharing several enjoyable days exploring the valley with me.

John Wilkinson
West Bretton
Spring 2002

The source of the River Dearne

CHAPTER ONE

Pre-History and Early Settlement

RISING IN THE TOWNSHIP OF CUMBERWORTH, the Dearne flows in a north-easterly direction until it reaches a point south of West Bretton. Here it turns to the south east, eventually joining the Don, and thence its waters are carried into the Humber. In its earliest stages it is joined by several small tributaries, arising in the townships of Flockton, Emley and Gunthwaite. The rocks of these upper reaches date from the Carboniferous Period. Geologists have shown that they were derived from older rocks that lay many miles to the north and north-east of the district, some 350 million years ago. Ancient rivers carried sedimentary materials from the rocks and deposited them on a huge delta which covered most of what is now West and South Yorkshire. Over many centuries they turned into the millstone grit which predominates in the valley. Coal, which once played a very important part in the local economy, was formed from vegetation which grew on that delta. Flood-water, bacterial action, and pressure from further sediments, brought about the transformation during a period of some 30 million years. At a later stage, volcanic upheavals thrust up the Pennine hills causing the coal measures to dip in an easterly direction - outcropping in the valley (until they were worked out) and concealed underground further to the east.

The constantly eroding action of rain, ice, frost and streams has transformed the primeval landscape but left a number of hills where harder stone proved more resistant to the weathering process than softer clays. Cumberworth, Birdsedge and Woolley Edge provide fine examples of this evolution. Such 'edges' were to offer the building materials and coal seam outcrops which could be exploited and which led to the numerous quarries, mines, buildings and boundary walls which are distinctive features of the district.

When people first settled in the valley cannot be known with certainty. What is clear is that they did not construct their rudimentary shelters on the valley bottom. Marshy ground, with the possibility of flooding from an uncontrolled river, would have precluded that. On the hills, where the soil was reasonably well drained and suitable for some grazing and cultivation in forest clearings, and where watch could be kept for approaching marauders, the first settlements came into being. Evidence of Neolithic occupation (about 4,000 years ago) has been found at Castle Hill in Denby, and there is a strong possibility that the great hill of High Hoyland was the site of an Iron Age settlement (some 2,000 years ago).

Cumberworth (Cumbra's Enclosure) possesses one of the few Celtic place names in the upper reaches of the valley, though that is not to say that Celtic man did not visit and settle in other parts. The origin of that particular place-name is uncertain, but maybe lies in that era in which Britain was a province of the Roman Empire. The names of Emley (Emma's field), High Hoyland (High land on a ridge), and Cawthorne (a cold place with a thorn tree) probably date from the seventh or eighth centuries, when the district was invaded and settled by Angles. Also probably dating from this time are Clayton West (Farmstead on clay) and Scissett (Celia's farmstead). The centre of gravity of both of these settlements lies more within the valley, a fact which reflects their nineteenth century development.

In the ninth century, Danish Vikings entered Britain and, having penetrated inland from the North Sea, left their mark in the place-names of Denby (Danish Settlement), and Skelmanthorpe (Skelmar's farm). They were to be followed, in the tenth century, by Norwegian Vikings who, migrating from territory they had already settled in Western Britain, brought British slaves with them - possibly from the district of the modern Cumbria. Their presence is suggested in the names of West Bretton (British farmstead), Flockton (Floki's farmstead) and Gunthwaite (Gunnhildr's clearing).

No substantial evidence has been discovered relating to any of these people. Who were they? What did they look like? What was the pattern of their daily lives? We can only make conjectures in the light of evidence found in other parts of the country. Probably rough in appearance, barbaric in sport, and servile to their chiefs, they would have constructed their simple timber and thatch dwellings, scratched a living from the soil and, against amazing odds, maintained a continuity of settlement which, with only a few interruptions, has endured until the present.

What is quite definite is that, during the course of the eleventh century, many parts of the valley had been reduced to wasteland. The great survey of much of the country, known as the Domesday Book and produced for William the Conqueror in 1086, provides firm evidence of the sheer devastation caused by the Norman soldiers; not just in the Dearne valley but throughout much of Yorkshire. Strong willed and stubborn, the proud people of the North of England were not prepared to submit meekly to rule by 'Southerners' - let alone 'Foreigners'! Several of the valley's settlements faced the terrible reprisal of the Conqueror. Entries in Domesday show what this meant in economic terms:

Settlement	Value before the Conquest	Value in 1086
Cawthorne	40 shillings	20 shillings
Clayton West	20 shillings	Waste
Cumberworth	6 shillings	Waste
Denby	10 shillings	6 shillings
Flockton	20 shillings	Waste
High Hoyland	20 shillings	5 shillings
Skelmanthorpe	80 shillings	Waste

Two other things may be learned from Domesday - that the Danish settlement at Denby was the only place in Yorkshire stated to possess a cattle farm ('Vaccary'), and that most of the valley had been granted by the Conqueror to his cohorts - the De Lacis, lords of the Honour of Pontefract, whose chief residence was at Pontefract Castle. Only parts of the Cumberworth, Emley, Flockton and West Bretton townships remained outside that gift, and were retained in direct royal ownership as part of the extensive Manor of Wakefield.

Such transactions probably made very little difference to the common peasant, who would have tried to live as he had always done, but with an extra struggle to maintain his lifestyle in the face of such destruction. He would have continued to offer his allegiance and dues to lesser and more local lords. Men like Ailric, Ukile and Godric, whose fiefdoms covered much of the valley, seem to have maintained their positions throughout the tempests of the eleventh century, even though they were themselves now required to offer various obligations to William's greater lords. Local they might have been, but they were still sufficiently powerful to strike fear into the heart of a peasant who forgot his station in life, for this was a distinctly hierarchical society. Not for the lowest of the low was there a right to question why each week or month he was required to perform hours of unpaid service on the land of someone who was more privileged than himself, whilst struggling to feed his own family at the same time. Not for him, unlettered and uninformed as he was, could there be much opportunity to actively resist the many demands of the lord's court as it regulated both his personal and social life and the life of the whole community in numerous ways.

CHAPTER TWO

Medieval Life

LIFE IN THE VALLEY in the post-Domesday era, and indeed for long afterwards, was centred on agriculture and its related crafts - as surviving deeds, wills and inventories make clear. In spite of the burdensome obligations owed by peasants to their lords, together with the constant fighting of a battle with the elements as land was tilled and crops grown, the economy appears to have successfully overcome the Norman devastation in a fairly short period of time. Population steadily increased, new and more substantial buildings were erected, and more land had to be taken into cultivation.

From the thirteenth century, under the overall direction of the local lords, waste and woodland were being encroached upon and ploughed up in a process known as 'assarting'. This was done with some caution, for the waste provided opportunities for sport and hunting, materials for building, and a pantry of acorns for village pigs. By law, assarted land had to be enclosed. Thus, a fringe of enclosures, usually irregular in shape, grew up around older, unenclosed, fields. Many still exist, frequently bearing the medieval name 'royd' (woodland clearing) in conjunction with a personal name. An extensive collection of fourteenth century deeds relating to West Bretton has been preserved and published by the Yorkshire Archeological Society, and provides a glimpse into this kind of development. There is mention of three unenclosed fields: the North Field, the South Field and the West Field, each containing several strips ('selions') cultivated by various tenants. There are also references to meadows, pastures, common land, and woodland - as well as to assarts.

The astute observer may find in the landscape some physical signs of the medieval farmer's activities. In the fields surrounding the farmstead of Bentley Grange in the Emley townships, beneath the spoil left by later ironstone mining, are the remains of selions of many centuries ago. Surrounding the village of West Bretton are several 'royds', long since isolated from any surrounding woodland. Later industrial activity, twentieth century open-cast coal mining, and the intensive farming methods of recent years have obliterated much evidence elsewhere.

In 1297, a tax was levied on the country's population as a way of raising revenue for King Edward I. The returns provide a revealing insight into the the kinds of crops being grown and the livestock being reared. Within a system which was essentially community farming, individual holdings were clearly very small in comparison with modern times and presumably provided food only for the people who were working them. (Possibly the tax collectors did not know the full story!) Amongst the recorded taxpayers were:

Place	**Name**	**Livestock**	**Cereals**
Cumberworth	Adam Brown	2 cows	6 quarts of oats 1 estirk (calf)
Emley	Willelmus Ingrani	4 oxen 1 horse 1 cow 8 sheep	1/2 qt of wheat 8 quarts of oats
Emley	Richard Cosyn	1 ox 1 horse 1 cow 4 sheep	4 quarts of oats
Flockton	Simon de Gren	1 ox 1 horse 1 cow	4 quarts of oats
Flockton	Michael de Flokton	2 oxen 1 horse 1 cow 10 sheep	4 quarts of oats
West Bretton	Ricardus, son of Hugonis	1 horse 2 oxen 6 sheep	6 quarts of oats

A very important adjunct to agriculture was a village's water-powered cornmill. This was provided by the local lord and all his tenants were required to take their grain to be ground there and pay quite heavily for the facility. Woe betide them if they dared to keep hand querns for use at home! Such mills were recorded in the thirteenth century in Cawthorne, Clayton West, Emley, Flockton, Gunthwaite, Skelmanthorpe, and on the Haigh boundary of West Bretton

Within most communities were people who combined subsistence farming with some kind of craft. References to potters in Emley in 1218-19 suggest that the fireclay found in association with coal seams in the district was even then being exploited. Tax Returns of 1379 show that there was a 'smith' in West Bretton, and two 'smiths' and several shoemakers in Cawthorne - a village which also appears to have contained a significant tanning industry. By 1418 an iron smithies, powered by a water wheel, was functioning at Clayton West, and a forge was located at Cawthorne.

The most significant development in the medieval life of the valley, however, was the arrival in the twelfth century of Cistercian monks

The remains of ironstone mining at Bentley Grange. Begun by monks from Byland Abbey, the mines passed into the hands of lay proprietors at the time of the Reformation. By the mid seventeenth century the seam was virtually worked out and production ceased.

from the North Yorkshire Abbeys of Byland and Rievaulx. Having set up 'granges' (i.e. monastic estates) in the townships of Emley and Flockton, they went on to become enterprising breeders of sheep and were permitted to graze large numbers of their animals, together with cattle, in Emley, Flockton and West Bretton. The flourishing English woollen trade of that time, exemplified in the woolsack of the Lord Chancellor, drew some of its imput from the valley. But there was more. Passing beneath the monastic grazing lands was a rich seam of ironstone, and from the twelfth to the fourteenth centuries, the monks thoroughly exploited this. The Byland grange at Bentley, on the outskirts of Emley, became a hive of industrial activity, and the remains of its bell pits may still be seen. Sunk to a depth of about six metres, the pits were worked outwards from the bottom of the shaft, so gradually creating a bell shape, until there was a risk of collapse. When that stage was reached the shaft was abandoned and another one sunk further along the seam. The extracted ore was smelted in a furnace near to the present Bank Wood, the fuel being charcoal produced from the surrounding woodland. Amongst the many valuable offshoots of this industry were the construction of roads and the enclosure of land. In 1237 the Byland monks were given legal right, by the local lord, to quarry stone in Emley for such purposes.

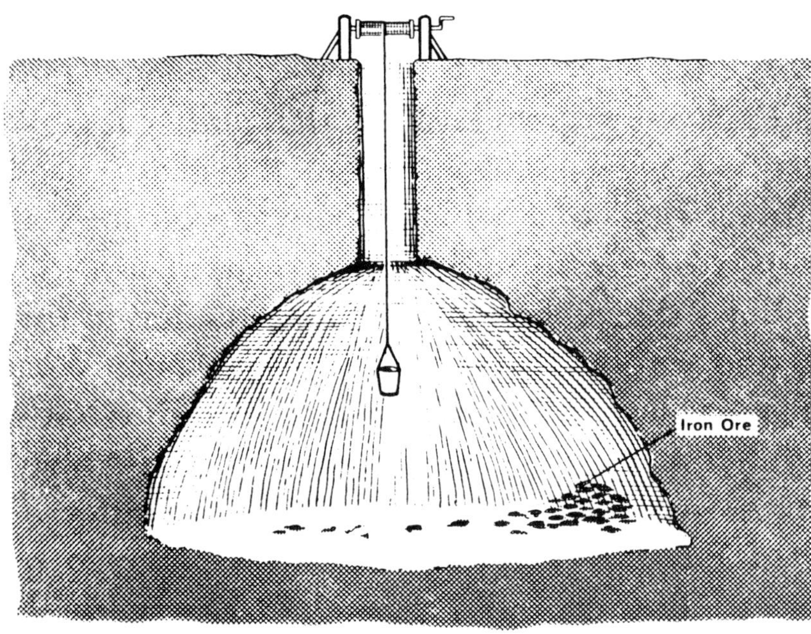

Diagram of a bell pit

The most important settlement in the valley in medieval times was Emley, a direct result of the monastic activity taking place within its boundaries. In 1253 Sir Thomas FitzWilliam, the local lord, was granted a royal charter giving him the right to hold a weekly market on Thursdays and an annual fair:

> every year for five days, that is to say on the Vigil and Feast of the Finding of the Holy Cross and three days following .....

At this market the monks would have been able to trade and the economy would have been boosted. The stage was in fact being set for Emley to develop into a prosperous town. It must be clear, however, to even the most casual of observers, that this never happened. A lack of a strong enough water supply for industrial purposes seems to have been the chief contributory factor and, only a few miles away, Huddersfield was beginning to emerge as a textile centre. There was a plentiful supply of water, and a gradual influx of weavers and accompanying craftsmen. So the wool trade moved from Emley, leaving the sheep grazing in the fields as before - but within a settlement that had quickly reached its peak and then declined in importance.

In the fourteenth century, the valley was struck by a catastrophe of the most serious proportions. The Bubonic Plague, or Black Death, which had been raging on the continent, entered England and somewhere between one half and one third of the country's population died. In many places there was terror and desolation. People did not understand the causes of the plague and, knowing no cure, were helpless in resisting its menacing advances. By 1350 it had entered the Dearne Valley. It seems certain that one consequence was that the monks in Emley and Flockton suffered greatly and that much of the valley's agricultural activity was decimated. The Manor of Emley was stated to be:

> ... lying waste for lack of tenants, owing to the pestilence.

Much of what had been achieved, both socially and economically, met a set-back that was to take many years to overcome. Indeed, the monastic activity never fully recovered, though it was to continue on a reduced scale until the dissolution of the monasteries in the sixteenth century. Thereafter, it passed into the hands of lay-people until, by the seventeenth century, the ironstone was virtually exhausted.

In one sense the plague may be counted as a mixed blessing. It seems to have weakened some of the burdening shackles of the old feudal system. A smaller workforce had to be offered more generous terms. Wages and money rents slowly took the place of ancient servile obligations. The valley moved into an era of tenant farmers and hired labourers who were still deferential to their lords and still dependent upon them in various ways, but not so thoroughly bound to them as had previously been the case. So it continued until the late eighteenth and early nineteenth centuries, when the wholly rural and agricultural nature of the valley began to change.

CHAPTER THREE

Industrial Growth and Decline

QUITE APART FROM THE MONASTIC ACTIVITIES in Emley and Flockton, other examples of rudimentary industrial activity had developed in the valley by Elizabethan times. Coal was being mined, on a small scale, in Clayton West and Emley by the sixteenth century, and in Cawthorne and Cumberworth a century later. Some brick making and the manufacture of pottery (albeit on a small scale) was to be found in West Bretton. Also, thriving iron furnaces were functioning in Cawthorne and West Bretton during the seventeenth and eighteenth centuries, though few signs remain of them.

The story of the valley's iron industry in the eighteenth century is one of a remarkable but short-lived enterprise. By 1730, every furnace and forge scattered over an area of some 45 square miles of the southern part of the West Riding of Yorkshire had come under the control of the great Spencer syndicate. The founding father was John Spencer, an astute Welsh maker of hayrakes, who came to Cawthorne in 1660 and married the heiress to the Cannon Hall Estate. By the latter years of the eighteenth century the industry began to decline. Charcoal fuelled furnaces were becoming increasingly old fashioned. Charcoal itself was expensive, and an alternative fuel in the form of coke had been developed by the Darby family of Coalbrookdale in Shropshire. It was both cheaper and more efficient, as well as being more readily available than the declining woodland necessary for the production of charcoal. In the face of a need to modernise, the Spencer syndicate broke up. The Spencers retired to become country gentlemen at Cannon Hall, Cawthorne, and part of their empire, including the furnace at West Bretton, came under the control of the Cockshutt family of Underbank Hall near Wortley. By the 1820s, Bretton Furnace had ceased to operate and, shortly afterwards, its site had been incorporated into an extended park around the Hall.

By the eighteenth century, the spinning and weaving of wool had become well established features of life in several of the valley's villages. Largely a domestic industry in the first place, as surviving examples of weavers' cottages make clear, a number of clothiers had built small warehouses in Skelmanthorpe by 1760. Fulling and scribbling mills were functioning in Denby Dale and Scissett around the same time, being powered by the water of the Dearne river. Then, during the second half of the eighteenth century, in common with much of the West Riding, this industry became an integral part of significant industrial expansion.

It has already been shown that the Dearne valley lies in the exposed area of the Yorkshire Coalfield, and it is hardly surprising that coal became one of the most important ingredients in the industrial expansion. By the 1700s it had become possible to do more than sink small bell pits on seam outcrops. Shafts could now be sunk to a depth

A small coalmine in Denby Dale in the early years of the twentieth century.

The former Emley Moor Colliery, c.1980.

of some 300 metres and local landowners were becoming sufficiently aware of new possibilities of creating wealth by issuing mining leases to interested prospectors. Towards the middle of the nineteenth century the industry grew dramatically, the advent of the steam engine for both factory and transport providing the main impetus. In 1865 some eleven mines were producing the precious fuel – at Cawthorne, Clayton West, Cumberworth, Denby Dale, Emley Moor, Emley Park, Flockton, Haigh and West Bretton. Several of these mines did not have a very long life, and most of them had closed by the end of the century, leaving behind only relics of their existence. Those that remained were Emley Park (later known as Park Mill) and Emley Moor, together with more recent developments in West Bretton and a small privately-owned mine in Scissett. All, except the Scissett mine, have now gone.

Amongst the mining entrepreneurs were members of the Milnes family of Flockton and the Lister Kayes who lived at Denby Grange, just outside the same village. The Milnes family had previously been timber merchants and maltsters – with little mining experience but a canny realisation of the possibilities it presented. With their growing prosperity they built for themselves a commodious residence in Flockton, grandly named the Manor House. Three brothers – Robert, Matthew and James Jagger – freeholders in Emley, began to prospect in Emley, Flockton and West Bretton in 1839. Edward Stringer – a wealthy gentleman-farmer of Emley Woodhouse – gave up farming on inheriting £60,000 from his father and began to develop the Park Mill Colliery. His descendants remained as colliery owners until the nationalisation of the industry in 1947. The Norton family of Scissett, who were primarily involved in textiles, sank mines in Clayton West in order to obtain fuel for their mill.

The expansion of the textile industry presents a similar story, in which a few adventurous entrepreneurs seized the opportunitites that raw materials, expertise and new industrial techniques provided. In Skelmanthorpe in 1770 John Field, a clothier of Gill Gate, became the founding father of a dynasty which developed a thriving trade in worsted products and which was highly flourishing until well into the twentieth century. In 1825 Joseph Norton, a small clothier, purchased Highbridge corn mill on the banks of the Dearne to the south of Skelmanthorpe and founded Nortonthorpe Mills. As his business grew it became necessary to employ more people and, since the particular 'fancy' trade that he was engaged in required weavers to be closely supervised by the designers, Norton decided to build cottages for his workforce near to his mill. Thus the village of Scissett developed in a valley that could now be drained and made habitable. Nearby, in Denby Dale, in the 1850s, Zechariah Hinchliffe expanded his worsted business and Jonas Kenyon began to manufacture fancy cloth for waistcoats. In 1869, Robert Beanland set up his spinning business in Clayton West alongside some six other textile manufacturers. In fact Clayton West was one of the villages considered by the future Sir Titus Salt as a site for his alpaca mills before going on to establish Saltaire to the north of Bradford.

Other industries that developed during the nineteenth century included the manufacture of bricks and drainpipes in Cumberworth and Denby Dale, and engineering and rope-making in Clayton West.

What had been rather insignificant rural hamlets steadily became communities of some substance, as the nineteenth century census returns make clear:

Township	**Population**					
	1801	**1831**	**1851**	**1871**	**1891**	**1901**
Emley	1,120	1,445	1,706	1,275	1,406	1,421
Flockton Chapelry	800	995	1,040	1,116	1,213	1,251
Clayton West *(including parts of Scissett)*	668	887	1,566	1,531	1,541	1,550
Cumberworth *(including parts of Scissett and Skelmanthorpe)*	1,805	2,554	4,067	4,414	4,895	4,851
Denby *(including Denby Dale)*	1,061	1,295	1,709	1,637	1,661	1,765

Closely intertwined with industrial growth, and without which such growth would have been impossible, was the development of an adequate transport system that would enable raw materials to be brought to the new mills and finished products to be sent to such trading centres as Huddersfield, Wakefield, Barnsley and Sheffield. The older roads, which meandered along the hill tops and occasionally crossed the valley by means of packhorse bridges, may have provided the inhabitants with splendid views (as they still do), but they were wholly unsuitable for the increased traffic that industry generated. From Tudor times, roads had been the responsibility of the residents of the parishes through which they passed, and since those residents were often (and understandably) reluctant to pay for and carry out repair work, they were little more than cart tracks, riddled with potholes and impassable at certain times of the year. The construction of turnpike roads by companies of trustees, who were enabled to charge tolls at various points along them, was an attempt to provide a more effective system.

The first turnpike road to be constructed in the valley linked Barnsley with Grange Moor, passing through West Bretton and Flockton. Built under an Act of Parliament of 1759, it connected at Grange Moor with the Wakefield-Austerlands turnpike which ran from Wakefield through Huddersfield and the Colne Valley to Manchester. In the same year, Cawthorne became similarly linked with Barnsley, so having access to an outlet for the products of its coal and iron industries. In 1776, a road was built between Huddersfield and Penistone, passing through the western extremity of the valley. It was not, however, until the 1820s, that the low-lying parts of the valley began to experience the benefits of this new mode of communication. In 1824 a turnpike was opened from Cawthorne, skirting Denby Dale and thence climbing the Pennines to Holmfirth and Lancashire. In 1825 the system was completed with the construction of a link between Wakefield and

The former nineteenth century toll keeper's cottage on the edge of West Bretton, built at the point where the Barnsley-Grange Moor turnpike (right to left) was crossed by the Wakefield-Denby Dale turnpike. From the 1920s the crossroads increasingly became a notorious accident spot. To alleviate the situation the cottage was demolished in 1954, and the large roundabout now to be found there was constructed in the 1970s.

Denby Dale. Passing through Clayton West, Scissett and Denby Dale, it was petitioned for by most of the leading gentry and industrialists in the area, and helped to ensure that these villages developed and industry flourished within them.

A further boost to industrial development came about a quarter of a

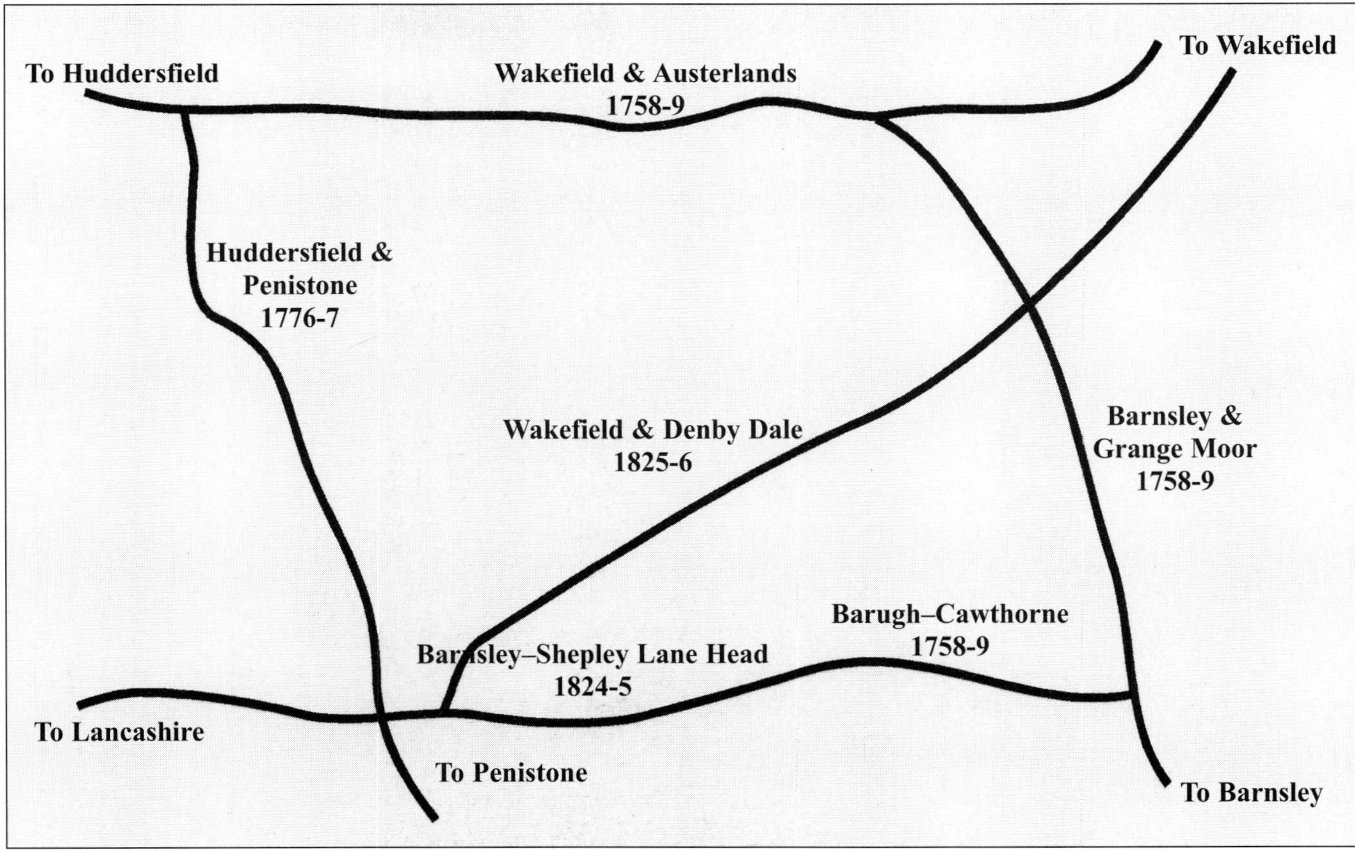

Turnpike roads in the Valley with dates of construction

century later with the construction of the Huddersfield and Sheffield Junction Railway, passing over a high wooden viaduct at Denby Dale - to be replaced by an even more impressive stone structure in 1880. The line was opened in 1850, and a branch line to Clayton West - with stations at Skelmanthorpe and Clayton West - followed in 1879. That branch line was closed in January 1983 but in November 1991 the old Clayton West station became the base of the Kirklees Light Railway, a 15" gauge line now providing for tourists rather than for industry.

The valley hardly saw the construction of canals - another important ingredient in the story of industrial expansion in the West Riding. Details in the archives of Bretton Hall show that plans were drawn for two, but neither one was built. One would have linked Barnsley with Wakefield, passing through Haigh and skirting east of West Bretton; and the other would have linked Emley with that. What had been intended as a branch of the Barnsley to Wakefield link was built from Barnsley to Cawthorne but, after considerable opposition had been encountered, the full link was constructed several miles to the east, right outside the valley.

It has been suggested that the working people of the Industrial Revolution were, in many ways, far more insecure than had been the lowly people of any previous age. Having been uprooted from the land, thus losing any degree of self-sufficiency, they were totally dependent on earning enough money to buy food, and they could only do this by selling their labour to factory owners who might exploit them. A measure of insecurity was felt within the valley from time to time and sometimes expressed itself in violence. In 1812, when food was in short supply, the Luddites were actively smashing factory machinery in the West Riding, believing that its introduction had put people out of jobs. Accompanying such destruction were food riots. The Military had to be placed on alert in Penistone and Barnsley, as well as in a number of local villages, in case corn mills should be plundered for food. It must also have become common knowledge that Bretton Hall, the seat of a rich, landed family, had to be protected from possible rioters.

Eight years later, in 1820, a further groundswell of discontent was felt in many of the textile villages around Barnsley and Hudderfield. Concerned about supposed oppression of the poor, unjust taxation, and the corruption of government ministers, leading radicals made plans for a great assembly at Grange Moor, to the north of the valley. It was hoped that many hundreds of disaffected men would gather, drawn from all over the North of England, and then march via Barnsley and Sheffield to London. In the event only about 300 turned up, and when rumours of government retaliation began to circulate, the men scattered - frightened and disheartened.

During the late 1830s and into the 1840s, at a time of economic depression, the Chartists, with their desire for better living conditions to be brought about through working-class control of Parliament, received some support in Skelmanthorpe. A banner that had been carried by local men to rallies of political protestors from 1819 onwards, and was carried to Chartist meetings, has been preserved in Huddersfield's Tolson Museum, and a public house in the village preserves the memory of radical demands in being called The Chartist.

When Parliament rejected the demands of the Chartists for the second time, in 1842, further unrest developed – at first in the Manchester area. Irate strikers conceived the idea of extracting plugs from factory boilers, thus bringing work to a complete standstill. Bands of angry 'plug rioters' marched over the Pennines to enlist support from their West Riding counterparts. On reaching Skelmanthorpe, they were provided with both sympathy and sustenance. Having refreshed themselves, they marched to Scissett and attempted to enter Joseph Norton's mill. Their mission came to nought since an alert cavalry was waiting for them and, after a reading of the Riot Act, the men were forced out of the valley.

Little seems to have been changed immediately by such demonstrations – though they perhaps helped to stimulate a gradual evolution in the understanding of man's place in society as the century proceeded. In fact the greater changes have come during the twentieth century and especially since the Second World War. Now the traditional industries of coal and textiles have lost almost all their significance. Only one (privately owned) coal mine remains in the valley. Industry has become a more varied scene in which engineering, the manufacture of pre-cast concrete items, and printing have made their appearance. But perhaps even more significant has been the discovery of the valley by the commuter. Whereas, during the nineteenth century, most working people were employed either within, or very near to, their own villages, most now travel to the larger urban centres around, and work in conditions that would have been no more than a dream to their predecessors. Gone are the days, still retained in some older memories, when sleepy men and women were summoned by the mill hooter in the early hours of the morning. The sophistication

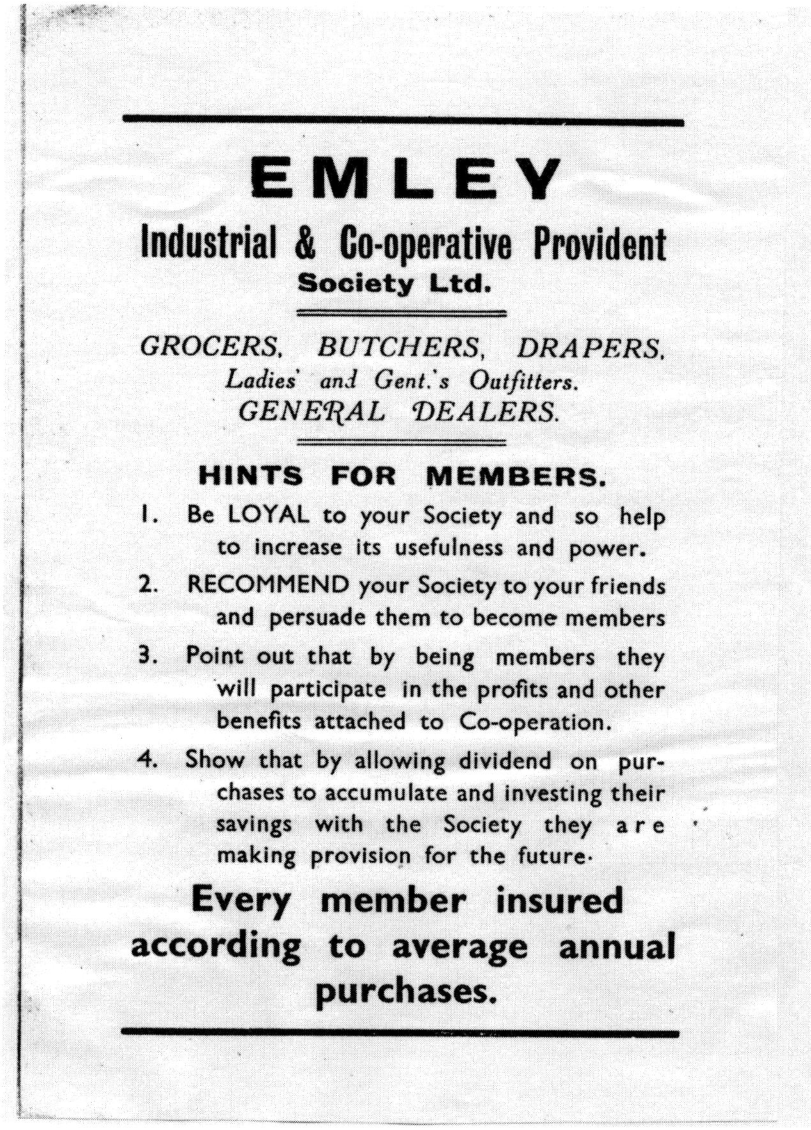

The Co-operative Movement was especially important to working-class people in the nineteenth and early twentieth centuries. Each industrial village in the valley had its 'Co-op' where goods of many kinds were sold at market prices, and surplus profits were divided amongst members in the form of the 'divi'. Most of these shops, in fact, continued until very recent times.

of alarm clock and petrol engine have become part of the general pattern of life. The former Wakefield to Denby Dale turnpike throngs each morning, not so much with vehicles carrying the products of industry, as with the mass of those who drive themselves away from the valley in their pursuit of economic viability.

The Barnsley-Shepley Lane Head turnpike road of 1824 at Cawthorne. What was once one of the toll-keeper's cottages has been converted into a commodious residence in recent times.

A valley farmstead circa 1900. Horse power was to last for about 50 more

CHAPTER FOUR

Agricultural Change

IT HAS BEEN ESTIMATED THAT, in the early eighteenth century, about four out of five of the nation's workforce was involved in agriculture. Much farming, both in the Dearne valley and in the country as a whole, was still at a subsistence level and increasingly being seen by some to be inefficient and wasteful. But rural tradition died hard. If the pigs of the villagers of Emley created mayhem when they roamed unringed through growing crops; if the residents of Cumberworth were, from time to time, reprimanded for putting:

> '... any scabbed or infectious horse on their common ....'

or, if the inhabitants of West Bretton were constantly being chastised by their manorial court for carelessness in maintaining hedges and fences, then so it had to be; lamentable maybe, but part of the perceived natural order of things.

By the end of the same century, however, several circumstances had combined to bring about a transformation in farming methods as well as in the appearance of large tracts of landscape. A rapidly growing population, especially in the new industrial centres, needed food; and to produce that food it was necessary to bring more land into cultivation. Imports from other countries were unreliable and slow and, especially during the Napoleonic era, easily interrupted. At the same time, more scientific methods of growing crops and breeding animals were being developed. People began to see that there were better ways of draining the land or sowing seeds, and a sensible rotation of crops (including newly introduced root and clover crops) meant that land did not have to lie in wasteful fallow from time to time to regain something of its wholesomeness. Such a rotation could best be organised, and crop diseases prevented from spreading, in enclosed fields rather than on numerous strips in the older open ones.

Much of the land in the valley had, in fact, been enclosed by 1800. In High Hoyland, total enclosure had taken place as early as 1684 and, in

West Bretton, the process was completed a century later at the same time as the Barnsley-Grange Moor turnpike was constructed across the remnants of the open common. There were still, however, pockets of waste, moor and common in several places which had been casually grazed from time immemorial by the livestock of village residents. In the early 1800s freeholders, under the leadership of their squires, petitioned Parliament to grant them the right to enclose these lands. So the commons of Skelmanthorpe, Denby and Cumberworth were enclosed under an Act of 1800, to be followed by Cawthorne Common in 1810 and Emley Moor in 1817. The neat regular shapes of the newly-created fields contrasts greatly with the haphazard patterns of the older enclosures.

The valley's principal landowners seem for the most part to have been favourably inclined towards change. It was almost certainly to their financial advantage to be so inclined. Indeed, through the written reports of the Board of Agriculture (founded in 1793) they were positively encouraged to believe that it would be to their ultimate advantage. One such report stated:

> The advantages of enclosing are great and manifold. The rent to the landlord is immediately raised at least one fourth ...

In 1794, Messrs Rennie, Broun and Shirreff described, in one of the Board's publications, what they had seen of farming on a tour of the West Riding. The villages of Emley, Gunthwaite and West Bretton had each been visited. The indications given in their writings are that what has become known as the 'Agrarian Revolution' had taken firm root and that progressive farming methods were being encouraged.

At Emley Woodhouse they found that wheat, peas and beans were being grown and had been sown with mechanical drills rather than by the previously wasteful scattering by a sower. A threshing machine was in use rather than the centuries-old flail.

In West Bretton, people were found to be 'sensible and industrious' and 'had a great turn to improvements ...' Several crop rotations were being practised, encouraged by the landowner; and dung, lime and bones were being applied to the land as fertilisers. Sheep were being reared (the Penistone breed being the most successful) and both threshing machines and Rotherham ploughs were in general usage. Farm units varied from 150 to 200 acres, which is little different from those of modern times.

In Gunthwaite, at the western end of the valley – where the climatic conditions tended to be perhaps a little harsher than in the east, and where communications were not quite so well developed – it was a rather different story. Smaller farms were discovered, consisting mainly of pasture and meadow and grazed by long horned Derbyshire cattle and Penistone sheep. The report indicated that the land in the Gunthwaite township needed draining, but that the proper method of doing it was not yet understood by the local inhabitants.

Comment was also made about the excellence of farm buildings, West Bretton being particularly singled out for mention. Many examples of seventeenth and eighteenth century buildings are still to be found throughout the valley. The former Home Farm of Bretton Hall provides one of the best illustrations of a thoughtfully planned and sturdily constructed farmstead – complete with house and a whole range of outbuildings. To them was added, in the early years of the nineteenth century, a splendid dairy which, though in a state of decay, preserves some of the magnificence of former years. Such farmsteads were designed to meet the needs of the farmer who both grew crops and kept livestock. They usually contained a barn in which corn was threshed, a range of livestock buildings where animals were kept in winter – and in which straw and hay were processed into manure – and a yard where the animals might be exercised and manure stored during winter months. Almost always it will be noticed that the yard lies on the southern side of the buildings and is protected by them from the prevailing winds.

During the nineteenth century, farming became increasingly mechanised. That fact, coupled with periods of agricultural depression caused by 'unchecked imports of cheap produce', meant less demand for human labour. A gradual movement of people from agricultural villages to industrial settlements, where a wider variety of employment was available, meant that the population of several of the valley's villages declined – a pattern which was to be continued during the first half of the present century. In 1801 the villagers of High Hoyland numbered 270; by 1951 they had been reduced to 139. Similarly in West Bretton 491 inhabitants were recorded in 1801, but only 316 in 1951. A careful study of the occupations listed in nineteenth century census returns for West Bretton, together with a survey of occupations represented in the same village in 1979, shows that the decline was directly related to agricultural change:

Occupations in West Bretton

	1841	1871	1979
Farmers	10	10	9
Agricultural Labourers	64	28	7

The late nineteenth century saw the beginning of quite a long period of agricultural depression which lasted until the 1930s. That fact, together with the outbreak of the two world wars, meant that few important developments took place, although the increasing use of tractors instead of horses was significant.

Since the 1950s, the story has been one of continual development – in expertise and mechanisation. On almost every farm in the valley are to be found the signs of the adaptation of resources. Mixed farming has given way to intensive beef and dairy production. Pigs, sheep or horses are rarities, apart from the occasional riding stable where young people are trained in the art of equestrianism. Farmsteads have begun to look more like factories for, surrounding the older buildings (usually constructed from locally obtained materials), are the silos and sheds of metal and concrete which furnish the required accommodation. In the fields, oats or wheat are rarely seen; barley is almost the only cereal grown, together with chemically fertilised grass for silage and strip grazing controlled by the electric fence. Occasionally, hedges, walls and fences have been removed to create larger fields which can be more comfortably negotiated by the combine harvester.

The village-based craftsmen, of whom there were many in the nineteenth century, have largely disappeared – for the modern farmer is both planner and engineer, and organises his work and resources in such a sophisticated way that the old crafts are rarely needed. In what has amounted to a second agricultural revolution, the rural habits of many years have come to an end. In some ways their loss may be regretted, but it is also true to say that a great deal of the misery and grinding work has gone and, in the process and in spite of occasional hiccups and health scares, a prosperity has developed which would have been totally beyond the wildest dreams of farmers of previous centuries.

CHAPTER FIVE

Developments in Personal Lifestyles

MANY IMPORTANT CHANGES have taken place in the style of everyday life since the beginning of the nineteenth century – more in the span of 100 years than had occurred for centuries beforehand. Several of these changes are closely intertwined, and the evidence of some may be seen through even the most cursory examination of the environment. Through an increase in educational opportunity, the development of more sophisticated forms of local government, and an enhancement of general living conditions, the valley's communities – as much as those in other parts of the country – have been transformed.

Education

The existence of at least one school in every village in the district provides evidence of an increasing recognition of the value of education, for whatever reason, during the nineteenth century. Compulsory education only became a feature of English life in 1880 but, for many years before that, small numbers of valley children were able to gain a limited literary and numerical insight by various means. Charity Schools, endowed by pious benefactors and providing some instruction in the 'Three Rs' and Biblical Knowledge were to be found in Denby Dale and Skelmanthorpe in the latter years of the eighteenth century. A similar (though possibly even more limited) programme was to be found in one or two 'Dame Schools'. Ephemeral and probably providing little more than a child-minding service, no written records of their activities appear to have survived.

A chantry school had been founded in Cawthorne as far back as 1454. Chantries were very much a feature of religious life in medieval times. They were founded, and financially endowed, primarily so that priests could regularly offer prayers for the souls of their deceased founders. They were a kind of celestial insurance policy! When chantries were suppressed during the turbulent years of Henry VIII's reign,

Cawthorne's school was refounded as a grammar school. Similar grammar schools were established in Emley and Flockton. All were short-lived. Within a century, the schools at Cawthorne and Flockton had become elementary schools – whilst that in Emley faded from the scene altogether, leaving behind only a few inscribed stones now tucked into the wall of the parish church's graveyard.

The first form of mass schooling in the nation came into being in 1808 when Joseph Lancaster, a Quaker, founded the British and Foreign Society to build and run elementary schools, Organised on a monitorial basis, and well supported by nonconformists, such schools appeared in many parts of the country. Surprisingly, in view of a significant nonconformist presence, only one British School appeared in the valley – in Emley. Opened in 1852, its building is still in use – now maintained by the Kirklees Local Education Authority.

A far stronger and more visible influence was to come after the formation of the National Society for the Education of the Poor in the Principles of the Established Church in 1811. Having a similar purpose and organisation to that of the British and Foreign Society, it placed an emphasis (as its cumbersome title made clear) on the provision of religious teaching from the point of view of the Church of England. Between 1816 and 1872, National Schools were founded in Cawthorne, Clayton West, Cumberworth, Denby, Emley, Flockton, High Hoyland, Scissett and Skelmanthorpe – and in West Bretton, the village school (which had been founded by the local lord of the manor in the eighteenth century) came under the auspices of the society.

For most of the nineteenth century this was the sum total of educational provision in the valley – but, by the 1860s, pressure was being mounted throughout the nation for a more vigorous State involvement in schooling. In 1870 an Education Act was passed by Parliament to 'fill up the gaps' in what had hitherto been the voluntary provision of schools. Local Boards were set up to build and maintain schools in those districts which were not already adequately provided for. Only a few such gaps remained within the valley – but they were to be filled. Financed partly by central government and partly from a locally levied rate, Board Schools were established in Clayton West, Denby Dale and Skelmanthorpe.

The influence of both voluntary and Board schools on the lives of individuals and communities is very difficult to assess. An examination of log books and attendance registers suggests that, in a mainly rural area, there was a degree of indifference and antipathy towards them –

which is shown in a significant absence of pupils for a variety of reasons, mainly connected with the demands of farming. On the other hand, it can hardly be doubted that they played a noteworthy part in raising standards of awareness. A former pupil of the British School at Emley in the opening years of the twentieth century has recorded his impressions of the elementary education he received. The curriculum included Arithmetic, Geography, the History of England to the time of the Tudors, Drawing, Essay-writing, English Literature, Music, Physical Education and occasional classes in Citizenship. Surrounding the teaching he recalled a liberal use of the cane, for which:

> the headmaster would have been put in gaol now.

Nevertheless, his considered judgement was that:

> although there was nothing elaborate about the education at Emley British School, it gave sufficient for a living to be made.

The story of educational development in the valley during the twentieth century is one of refinement and expansion. In 1902 the West Riding County Council took over responsibility for educational provision and was gradually able to bring an enlightened and resourceful approach to bear upon it. In 1944, a Secondary Modern school was opened at Scissett to cater for the needs of pupils who were, from the age of eleven, to receive a more specialised education than had hitherto been available. A few pupils travelled to Grammar Schools in Penistone, Wakefield, Ossett and Huddersfield (and to Holme Valley Grammar School when it was opened in 1932) having undergone selection examinations and been awarded scholarships.

In 1974, a comprehensive system was introduced which centred, for most of the valley communities, on the new Shelley High School built on the outskirts of Skelmanthorpe. The Secondary Modern school at Scissett became a middle school and the village schools were now known as First Schools.

Another significant educational enterprise was initiated in 1947 when Bretton Hall, the ancestral home of the Viscounts Allendale, was sold to the West Riding County Council and became a college for the training of teachers of music, art and drama. In more recent years it has diversified its courses on becoming a College of Higher Education, then a University College closely attached to the University of Leeds and, from 2001, fully integrated with the University. Through its various activities it has had a considerable influence throughout the valley and far beyond.

Local Government

From Tudor times local administration had been increasingly centred on the parish. Originally a geographical area served by a priest, it was seen to be a convenient unit for secular government. Yet, although the Parish Vestries – representing the local ratepayers – had the official task of appointing, or recommending for appointment to the County Justices of the Peace meeting in Quarter Session, such officials as churchwardens, constables, surveyors of the highways and overseers of the poor, arrangements were frequently confused and variable – and not only in the Dearne Valley. In following local tradition and custom, the Vestries lacked the competence that would be considered desirable in a modern, democratic society. In rural areas, the landed gentry wielded considerable powers over both their tenants and their neighbours. Alongside a minimum of parochial administration, there was a tendency for their manorial courts to regulate village life – and this continued in some places into the nineteenth century. The Wentworths of West Bretton, the Saviles of Rufford Abbey in Nottinghamshire (who were also the lords of Emley), the Bosvilles of Gunthwaite and the Spencers (later Spencer-Stanhopes) of Cawthorne, were landowners of considerable substance. People who depended on them for all aspects of their livelihood were understandably reluctant to do anything that might be construed as disloyalty.

As the nineteenth century proceeded, however, the old intertwined parish and manorial systems became manifestly inadequate – especially in villages where the population was increasing. A process of piecemeal rationalisation was therefore begun, which slowly led to greater efficiency and a more sensible accountability towards people who were gaining a greater say in how they were governed. Following the passing of the Poor Law Amendment Act of 1834, parishes were relieved of the direct and costly administration of poor relief with which they had been burdened for several centuries. Poor Law Unions and elected Boards of Guardians replaced Justices of the Peace and Parish Overseers. Most of the valley's communities now came within the orbit of the Wakefield and Penistone Poor Law Unions, and workhouses were established in both Wakefield and Penistone.

By an Act of Parliament of 1856, the West Riding Constabulary was created, thus taking from the parishes the direct responsibility for keeping the peace, and introducing the village 'Bobby'. By the permissive terms of an Act of 1839, such a force could have been set up some seventeen years earlier. But Yorkshire suspicion of centralisation, and an even greater fear of costs, had meant that nothing was done until it had to be.

Other local government bodies were steadily brought to birth – not so much out of an enthusiastic conviction that this was the right way forward, but because of a series of calamities. The Victorians came to see that there were close links between bad sanitary conditions, sickness, and the dreaded curse of pauperism. All were undesirable; none could be properly dealt with by the local parish officials. And so, as outbreaks of cholera, typhoid and other diseases occured, changes took place. Local Health Boards, with powers to cleanse, light and pave streets, had been provided for by the Public Health Act of 1848, and came into being in Skelmanthorpe and Emley in the 1860s and in Denby, Cumberworth and Clayton West in the 1870s. The more rural parts of the valley were brought under the jurisdiction of Rural Sanitary Authorities centred on Wakefield, Penistone and Kirkburton.

The records of all these authorities provide many illustrations of the difficulties caused in the Valley by open drains, inadequate sewage disposal, and outbreaks of infectious disease. Such problems were not easily or cheaply resolved. As late as 1898 the residents of Cumberworth had to be prohibited from emptying their chamberpots in the open streets. And in West Bretton, no proper sewage disposal facilities were constructed until the 1950s. The provision of gas-powered street lights and an adequate supply of piped water – replacing pumps and frequently contaminated wells and streams – together with the problems of repairing and widening unturnpiked roads in an area where industrial traffic was increasing, were matters of constant concern and placed such heavy financial burdens on local ratepayers that something more had to be done.

In 1889, the whole of the valley was brought under the jurisdiction of the West Riding County Council, a newly elected body under the terms of the Local Government Act of 1888. The County Council now took over responsibility for the police, major highway administration and repairs, and public health. From 1902, as has already been seen, it also assumed responsibility for education.

Six years later, in 1895, the remaining civil functions of parish vestries

WAKEFIELD

RURAL DISTRICT COUNCIL.

SCARLET FEVER.

ATTENDANCE AT SCHOOLS.

You are hereby informed that it is dangerous and contrary to the Law to send any Child to School until it is free from infection HOWEVER MILD THE CASE MAY BE.

No child living in a house in which there is a case of Scarlet Fever, should attend School or be allowed to play with other children, or go into any other house.

Infection continues until all trace of "peeling" has disappeared which rarely happens in less than SIX WEEKS from the date of the rash. The feet are usually the last to become clear.

J. J. JACKSON,
Medical Officer of Health.

CAUTION.

THE PUBLIC HEALTH ACT PROVIDES THAT

(1) Any person who while suffering from Scarlet Fever exposes himself without proper precautions against spreading the diseases in any STREET, PUBLIC PLACE (school), SHOP, INN, or PUBLIC CONVEYANCE; or

(2) Being in charge of any person so suffering so exposes such sufferer (or permits such exposure); or

(3) Gives, lends, sells, transmits, or exposes without previous disinfection any bedding, clothing, rags, or other things which have been exposed to infection from such disease

Shall be liable to a Penalty of £5.

In modern times it is rare to hear of children dying from such diseases as measles, whooping cough, diptheria and scarlet fever. All were common in the ninteenth and early twentieth centuries and it was partly to counteract their spread that Health Boards and Rural Sanitary Authorities were set up – later to be replaced by Urban and Rural District Councils.

were transferred to Parish Councils and Parish Meetings, and Rural and Urban District Councils came into being. The villagers of West Bretton – who now came within the jurisdiction of Wakefield Rural District Council – and of High Hoyland, Cawthorne and Gunthwaite – who were brought into the area served by Penistone Rural District Council – were able, for the first time, to elect their representatives to these bodies and to their local Parish Councils. At the same time, the Boards of Health of Clayton West, Denby and Cumberworth, Emley, and Skelmanthorpe were transformed into Urban District Councils with similar electoral provision. Under a further reorganisation in 1938, these four councils merged to create the Denby Dale Urban District Council.

By 1974, change was in the air again and another reorganisation of local government took place. Rural and Urban District Councils were abolished and the valley was apportioned between the Kirklees, Wakefield and Barnsley Metropolitan District Councils – as well as between the two new counties of West and South Yorkshire. Parish Councils continued in the smaller villages and the area formerly served by the Denby Dale Urban District Council was granted a similar facility. The larger units were to be a far cry from the old parish vestries with their immensely local and rustic concerns. Whilst they clearly could not be so immediately accountable to their electors, they could contain a far more sophisticated expertise.

More recently, in 1986, the County of West Yorkshire was abolished as an administrative unit and the Metropolitan District Councils became unitary authorities.

Living Conditions

Any appreciation of a locality is considerably enhanced by a study of its dwelling houses. All the valley's settlements contain houses of differing age, style, size and shape – which often say a great deal about local craftsmanship, economic standards at the time they were built, and changing lifestyles.

Readily available millstone grit with its strong durability, together with long-lasting oak wood, had provided the basic raw materials for masons and joiners to construct cruck-framed or box-framed buildings from late medieval times onward. Utilitarian their work may have been, yet it has gathered a charm which comes partly through maturity. Several such houses have been modified or rebuilt with the passage of time, retaining older timbers and stones which imaginative down-to-earth craftsmen could re-use. Examples of their work are to be found in Cawthorne and Denby Dale, and on the hills to the south of the village of Scissett.

By the seventeenth century, in what seems to have been an era of considerable building activity, it had become possible to build more substantial stone dwellings. Cottages of woolweaving families and of agricultural labourers, as well as the larger houses of yeomen farmers (of which there are particularly fine examples in Emley) were all alike fashioned from the local material. Only in West Bretton, where a seam of fireclay was conveniently sited for exploitation, were bricks used. An enterprising landowner was there able to establish on his estate a small kiln in which were fired the deep red bricks which have become such a pleasing aesthetic feature of that village and which continued in production until the latter years of the nineteenth century.

A further spate of building and rebuilding in the eighteenth century resulted in several new farm houses and one or two spacious mansions for the gentry. Surrounded by rolling parkland in the fashion of the time, houses like Bretton Hall and Cawthorne's Cannon Hall have become jewels of architectural style – and focal points of educational and leisure activities – since their owners discovered that they could no longer afford their upkeep.

Nineteenth century industrial expansion saw the appearance of many terraced houses in several of the communities – a stark contrast to the rural charms of older properties. Yet, not all of these were erected without careful and considerate planning. When Joseph Norton began to build houses for his workforce in Scissett, he was sufficiently enlightened to have the comfort of these people in mind. Almost anticipating the efforts of Sir Titus Salt in Saltaire, or of George Cadbury in Bournville, he tried to ensure that more than just basic facilities were provided. Each house was provided with its own well in a cellar, the overflow from one filling the next all along the line. The supply was drawn from a natural spring. Since it was not always reliable, he ensured that full rights of way were established to the river in order that people might, if necessary, draw their supply there. At a later stage, when it was discovered that much of the well water had seeped through a graveyard, he made provision for all the houses to be connected to a piped supply. He also insisted that each tenant should be provided with a pig-sty so that the family's diet might be supplemented with home-reared meat. Sadly, his elaborate plans never reached full fruition for, by the 1840s, his capital had been lessened by fluctuations in the fortunes of the textile trade.

With the coming of the railway, it became possible to import building materials from other parts of the country without prohibitive cost. Whilst there were many advantages in this, not least because locally quarried stone was not infinite, it served to stifle particularly local features and resulted in buildings which could be located almost anywhere in the country.

This move towards uniformity continued with gathering speed during the 1960s when the valley was discovered by the commuter. The development of a motorway network, together with commonplace car ownership, brought the valley within easy reach not only of fairly local urban centres like Barnsley, Huddersfield or Wakefield, but also the more distant cities of Leeds, Bradford, Sheffield and Manchester. People could work in these cities, but they now had the freedom and sufficient economic means to live considerable distances away from them. Every village in the valley provides evidence of their presence. Occasionally, this has resulted in some older property being sympathetically updated, but more often it has produced suburban-type housing which is totally devoid of 'localness'. Moreover, what had been quite distinct communities were brought closer together physically. The uninformed traveller found it increasingly difficult to discover where Clayton West and Scissett separated from each other, or where Skelmanthorpe actually became Skelmanthorpe.

A study of the sizes of gardens attached to houses reveals interesting evidence of a move away from a near self-sufficiency in the production of vegetables – which was an established feature of rural life for centuries – to an era of refrigeration and supermarkets. The large gardens of older properties slowly gave way to small plots and, in some cases, to unfenced grassland areas, broken only by carefully planted trees or cupressus-screened patios. What had been a significant and necessary part of the rural economy became a mere appendage – an area, not for serious food production, but for equally serious relaxation.

As Joseph Norton had provided his tenants with pig-styes, so, within some of the older cottage gardens, may be found the remains of the same kind of facility. The poorly paid rural dweller needed to supplement his meagre diet and lovingly tended his pig until it was of a sufficient size to be worth killing. Also to be seen at the bottom of some gardens are the relics of draughty and unhygienic privies – contrasting significantly with the centrally heated, tiled conveniences which have become accepted essentials of modern life.

Gas, electricity, piped water, telephones and adequate sewage-disposal facilities have all added to the general well-being of the valley's population, and have made their mark in the form of storage tanks, pylons, street lamps, kiosks and filter beds. It was only, however, in the years that followed the Second World War that most of the inhabitants began to enjoy most of these facilities. Several of the smaller villages never gained all of them. The minutes of the Parish Council of West Bretton reveal that the Wakefield Gas Company would have been happy to supply their fuel in 1911, but canny village councillors, mindful of any burdensome expenditure, rejected the suggestion. Ironically, some sixty years later, when much of the country was being connected to the natural gas of the North Sea, the Parish Council of the same village considered that it would be a good idea for their village to be so provided. The Gas Board gave their considered judgement that the work could not be carried out. It would have been too expensive!

CHAPTER SIX

The Place of Religion

THAT CHRISTIANITY HAS PLAYED A SIGNIFICANT PART in the thinking and practices of the people of the valley during many centuries is shown by numerous churches and chapels to be found in all its communities (though not now so many as would have been found some thirty years ago). When that influence first became apparent is shrouded by the mists of antiquity. What does seem clear is that, before there were any religious buildings, there was religious teaching. It seems likely that a Christian centre of some significance had been established at Dewsbury by the seventh century, and that itinerant priests may have journeyed from there into the valley – preaching and baptising, either in the open air or in rudimentary shelters.

The remains of an ancient stone cross from High Hoyland, now preserved in the Tolson Museum, Huddersfield.

Anglo-Saxon remains from High Hoyland Church, preserved in Huddersfield's Tolson Museum, indicate that a preaching place of some kind had been founded there by the eighth or ninth centuries – and portions of a stone cross in the graveyard at Cawthorne suggest that Christianity was also known of there in the same period. Across the valley, in Emley, Anglian grave-slabs and the remains of a tympanum built into the internal church wall are pre-medieval in date. Possibly the centuries-old dedication of the church at Emley to St Michael gives some evidence of an original pioneering stance in the spread of Christianity in Yorkshire. Many churches throughout Europe, possessing the same dedication, were for a long time on the borderline of Christendom. Those who fought to spread their faith beyond such a border claimed the protection of that saint.

Receptive to local customs and traditions, and able to relate to the annual cycle of the year's seasons (as well as to the traumatic moments of birth, marriage and death), ancient Christianity (a mixture of superstition and genuine piety) began to consolidate its hold on the valley people. Under the patronage of both greater and more local lords, a parish structure evolved which was to last until modifications were made in the seventeenth and nineteenth centuries. This structure bore little relation to the natural boundaries of the valley itself. High Hoyland and Emley were to be the only parish centres contained within the valley, and they embraced parts of the settlements at Scissett, Skelmanthorpe and Clayton West. Other parishes reaching into the valley included Penistone (in which Denby was included), Kirkburton (which incorporated some parts of Cumberworth), Silkstone (which embraced Cawthorne, other parts of Cumberworth, and some of West Bretton), Sandal Magna near Wakefield (which included portions of West Bretton) and Thornhill (of which Flockton was a chapelry). Cawthorne and Cumberworth were to become independent parishes in the seventeenth century.

Gradually, purpose-built churches of some substance replaced cruder and more temporary structures. By the middle of the twelfth century, stone buildings had been erected in Emley and High Hoyland. A century later, in the era of the village's economic prosperity, Emley Church was rebuilt and enlarged. Some time between 1158 and 1189 a chapel was built in Cumberworth under the patronage of the Dronsfield family (lords of both Cumberworth and West Bretton) whilst, in West Bretton itself, members of the same family erected a chapel-of-ease in 1358. A substantial church had been built in Cawthorne by the early thirteenth century, relics of which may be seen in the present, largely nineteenth century, building.

Some impetus may have been given to Christian advance by the presence of the Byland and Rievaulx monks in the Emley, Flockton and West Bretton settlements. It is known that, at Bentley Grange, the monks erected a chapel dedicated to St Werburgh – no trace of which now remains. This was a unique dedication. Werburgh, a seventh century abbess of Ely and patron saint of Chester, was the daughter of

King Wulfhere of Mercia. It is possible that the dedication was related to the fact that the Fitzwilliams, medieval lords of Emley, were connected by marriage to the Constables of Chester.

How far the cataclysm of the Reformation of the sixteenth and seventeenth centuries affected the lives of valley people is very difficult to estimate. Apart from such immediate changes as the dissolution of the monasteries, and the introduction into church services of the English language in place of Latin, many people were probably more bemused than estranged. For some, however, the changes proved quite devastating. John Bretton of West Bretton could not subscribe to the laws which gave birth to the Church of England. Having, as a consequence, been forced to flee from the district, and forfeiting most of his estates, he was executed in York in 1598 as an 'obstinate recusant'. Similarly, in Cawthorne, Denby and Emley, were other individuals who had to face the stigma of being labelled 'papist' and consequently considered as traitors.

On the other hand, as the seventeenth century developed, the more extreme form of Protestantism known as 'Puritanism' gained support in the valley. Having read their Bibles and some of the writings of continental reformers, the Puritans decided that changes had not been far-reaching enough for their liking. Some remained within the Church of England, hoping to reform it from within. The Bosvilles of Gunthwaite Hall were one such family. In 1627, Godfrey Bosville built a chapel-of-ease in Denby for the benefit of parishioners who were finding it difficult to travel to their parish church in Penistone, and he ensured that the curate appointed was a man of Puritan sympathy. Others found, however, that their reforming zeal meant that they were pushed out of the Established Church. In 1662 the Rev. Robert Inman, the Rector of High Hoyland, was ejected from his living, though he continued to live in Clayton West until his death and there prepared the way for subsequent nonconformist activity.

By the end of the seventeenth century a Quaker society, representing almost the most radical of the religious groups of the Reformation, was meeting at High Flatts. A converted barn served as their headquarters – a building which is still in use. Presumably their congregation was drawn from a considerable area, for there are references to isolated Quaker families in several of the villages in Visitation Returns of the Diocese of York.

The golden era for the Protestant nonconformists in the valley dawned, however, in the nineteenth century. Population movements into the rising industrial centres of Clayton West, Denby Dale, Scissett and Skelmanthorpe rendered the existing parochial system of the Church of England quite inadequate to cope with the spiritual needs of people. Parish Churches like High Hoyland became remote from the hub of human activity. Like boats keeled over on a beach following the ebb of the tide, they were left high and dry. Where a spiritual vacuum was in danger of developing, the nonconformists stepped in – providing a warm, 'simple' faith and much opportunity for active lay participation. Throughout the valley, the spread of their societies began, starting with the Independents at Clayton West who were meeting from about 1794, the Independents at Flockton in 1802, and the Baptists of Clayton West in 1824.

Even more influential was the rise of Methodism – at first a purifying movement within the Church of England – developing into a separate denomination on the death of its founding father, John Wesley, in 1791 – and later splitting into a number of sub-groups. Several of these sub-groups took root in the valley. In 1760, Wesleyan Methodists were meeting in Flockton and, in spite of much opposition from the Rector, had gained a foothold in Emley by 1776. Denby Dale saw the formation of a society in the 1790s and Cawthorne, Clayton West and Skelmanthorpe by the opening years of the nineteenth century. Such societies usually began as cottage-meetings before developing the confidence and accumulating the resources to erect purpose-built chapels. In Denby Dale, the first Methodist services were conducted in a textile mill belonging to John Wood (a convert to the movement), whilst in Skelmanthorpe the Town School was used. Generally, it became easier for the movement's followers to erect their own buildings in those villages like Skelmanthorpe and Clayton West (where there was no one dominant landowner) than in tightly knit estate villages like West Bretton, where landowners were usually quite lacking in sympathy towards them and could prevent them from purchasing land.

By the 1790s, the Wesleyan Methodists were torn asunder in some parts of the country by the followers of Alexander Kilham, a minister who was expelled by the Methodist Conference for his radicalism – in particular for advocating a greater lay participation in the movement's affairs. The effects of the ensuing agitation were particularly felt in the Huddersfield district, and it is hardly surprising that it spilled over into the valley. Considerable numbers of members seceded and founded what was to become known as the Methodist New Connexion. In

Clayton West, Cumberworth, Denby Dale, Emley, Haigh and West Bretton, the new movement's adherents met.

Again, when Primitive Methodism began to spread through the North of England, the people of the valley were often responsive to its ideals. A charismatic development, deliberately using the title 'Primitive' as an indication of a supposed return to the original ideals of Methodism (which, it was felt, had become lost with the passage of time), it had a particular appeal to working-class people. Between 1819 and 1850 its societies were established in Clayton West, Cumberworth, Denby Dale, Emley, Flockton, High Hoyland, Skelmanthorpe and West Bretton.

Amongst other nonconformist groups that appeared in the valley were the Wesleyan Reformers – another break-away movement from Wesleyan Methodism – which began in 1849 and whose adherents formed societies in Birdsedge, Cumberworth, Clayton West, Denby, Denby Dale, Emley and Skelmanthorpe. Then, in 1884, a corps of the Salvation Army was founded in Denby Dale. In 1907 General William Booth, the Army's founder, visited the village and was greeted by large crowds.

Thus, by the dawn of the twentieth century, the religious life of the valley was both vigorous and complex. A strong (though divided) nonconformity competed for the allegiance of people with a Church of England that had increasingly been forced to recognise a need for its own reformation. As far back as the 1830s the parish of Scissett (including Skelmanthorpe township) had been carved out of parts of the parishes of Emley and High Hoyland, and a new church building was consecrated. Flockton had acquired parochial status in 1860, becoming independent of its mother church at Thornhill. All Saints Church in Clayton West was consecrated in 1875, the rights of a parish church being transferred to it from the isolated High Hoyland building. High Hoyland Church itself continued in occasional use until 1980, when it was declared redundant and sold for conversion into a hostel. In 1893 a church was built at Denby Dale within the parish of Cumberworth – and this was followed, two years later, by St. Aidan's Church in Skelmanthorpe. Skelmanthorpe became an independent parish in 1900.

A pattern of ecclesiastical organisation had emerged which has continued, with only minor modifications, up to the present time. Some churches and chapels disappeared as result of denominational unions (especially within Methodism), some because of a decline in the numbers of members, and others were rebuilt or restored. Old rivalries, which were frequently a feature of Victorian and Edwardian church life, have become largely irrelevant and almost forgotten. Nowhere is this better illustrated than in the village of West Bretton, once an establishment-orientated estate village in which denominational differences engendered considerable tension and misunderstanding. There, in 1982, Anglicans and Methodists joined together in one pioneering congregation and created what is officially known as a 'Local Ecumenical Partnership'.

Exploring the Villages

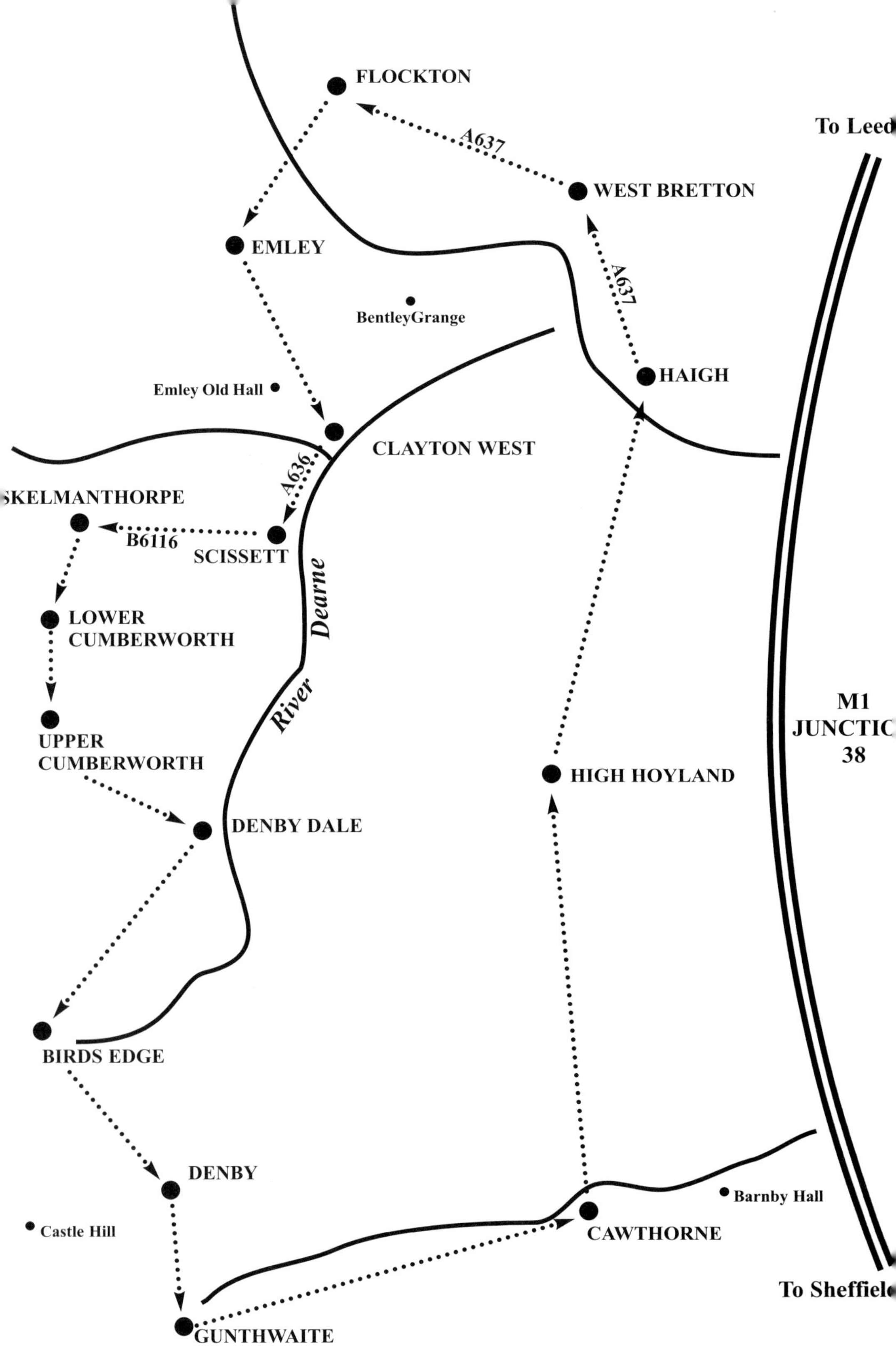

The Villages in the Upper Dearne Valley

West Bretton

SITUATED ON THE A637, the former Barnsley to Grange Moor turnpike, the village was the centre of a considerable rural estate for almost 900 years and has retained several features of such a settlement – the hall, the estate office, the home farm, and cottages of former estate workers.

In the thirteenth century, the ownership of the village passed from a family known simply as De Bretton into the hands of a family called variously Dronfield, Dronfeld or Dransfield, of whom little is known. After the death of Sir William Dronfield, the last of the male line, in 1406, the greater part of the property was inherited by his sister, Agnes, who had married into the influential Yorkshire family of Wentworth, and it remained with her descendants for almost four centuries. With the death in 1792 of bachelor Sir Thomas Blackett (the last of the Wentworths of Bretton, who had changed his surname on inheriting property in Northumberland from his mother's family – the Blacketts), West Bretton passed to one of his illegitimate daughters, Diana, wife of Lt Col Richard Beaumont, MP for Northumberland and a member of another old Yorkshire family. Five generations of Beaumonts lived at West Bretton, becoming prominent in the public life of the nation and ennobled with a barony in 1906, followed by a viscountcy in 1911. They took the title Allendale from part of the estates they owned in Northumberland. Heavy maintenance costs, aggravated by military occupation of the Hall during the 1939-45 War, led to it being sold to the former West Riding County Council in 1947 - to be followed, some ten years later, by the remainder of the Estate.

Bretton Hall was sufficiently important to be mentioned on Christopher Saxton's map of Yorkshire in 1577. Of that particular building there are now no visible remains, though some Tudor woodwork and a four-poster bed (reputedly built for Henry VIII to sleep in during the course of one of his northern tours) have been preserved at Temple Newsam House in Leeds.

The mansion, as it now stands, is a mixture of age and architectural style – and includes a pre-eighteenth century building which has been totally remodelled: the main mansion dating from about 1720 (erected in a century that was noteworthy for the rebuilding of large country houses) and a connecting link between the two, built about 1815 and formerly containing a library, dining room, music room and orangery. Nearby are the former stable and coach house – designed by George Basevi, the architect of the Fitzwilliam Museum in Cambridge. More recent buildings provide the accomodation required by a higher education institution.

Surrounding the hall is the former parkland, the result of a vast landscaping exercise in the second half of the eighteenth (and through much of the nineteenth) century. The fashion of the day was being followed. The increased possibility of foreign travel, for those who could afford it, introduced wealthy landowners to European culture including the classical landscape paintings of Claude and Poussin. The desire to create landscaped parks which imitated their style became very strong. Fussy ornamental gardens disappeared, and in came grassland and trees. The emphasis was on trying to create a natural rather than a man-made look. Bretton Park is very much in the style of William Kent or 'Capability' Brown – the great landscape architects – but it appears to have received some imput from a slightly lesser-known though capable man, Richard Woods, who also advised John Spencer on the laying out of the grounds at Cannon Hall in Cawthorne.

Within the Park are several interesting features: the lakes, formed by throwing a dam across the Dearne; a number of ha-has (sunken walls hidden from view and providing boundaries which do not intrude on the landscape); and the remains of Bretton Furnace. A few metres from the entrance to the present Bretton Country Park, irregular grassy slopes and hillocks of metallic residue – together with the line of a former water course – are all that can now be seen. Sparse though these remains are, they are, nevertheless, the only surviving example of a former charcoal-fuelled blast furnace to be found in West Yorkshire.

Today, the park is a much-used public facility. On 24th September 1977, the grounds immediately surrounding the Hall – together with the former kitchen gardens – became home to the Yorkshire Sculpture Park – the first permanent sculpture park in Great Britain. In June 1978 the City of Wakefield Metropolitan District Council, in association with the Countryside Commission, bought the former park for £132,000 to create a Country Park. The declared intention was that the development of such a facility would maintain and enhance the high landscape quality of the area,

Bretton Hall as it appeared in the 1920s – The South Front

A view from the east showing the main entrance in the eighteenth century building covered by a portico added in the early nineteenth century.

Sir Thomas Blackett of Bretton Hall
1725-1792
The last member of the Wentworth family to live at West Bretton, he changed his surname o inheriting considerable wealth from his mother's family, the Blacketts, who were prosperou merchant traders in Northumberland. He was a generous benefactor to the village and wa largely responsible for initiating the creation of the parkland around the Hall.

as well as permit members of the public to gain regular access and enjoyment of it.

On the edge of the Country Park stands the former Chapel-of-Ease of St. Bartholomew. Built in 1744 for Sir William Wentworth it replaced a medieval building on another (undiscovered) site. Of classical style, with a curious 'pepper pot' tower and a fine Venetian window at its east end, it was planned as a chapel-of-ease rather then a parish church. West Bretton was originally divided between the ecclesiastical parishes of Sandal Magna and Silkstone, as has already been stated, and this particular building, as well as its predecessor, was erected as a chapel for the landed family of Bretton Hall and for the convenience of their tenants who would otherwise have had to make long and arduous journeys to reach their parish

The former chapel of ease of Saint Bartholomew in Bretton Park.

The War Memorial in West Bretton, unveiled on 23rd October 1921. Built by Estate stone masons, it cost £185 18s 10½d. Built with stone taken from the site of an old menagerie in Bretton Park, it has a shape which is, perhaps, unparalleled by any other War Memorial in the country.

churches. The chapel remained in private ownership until 1956, when it was given by Viscount Allendale to the diocese of Wakefield. In 1995, having been declared redundant as a worship centre, it was sold to Bretton Hall College. Immediately to the east of the building is an enclosed area of the graveyard in which are buried all the owners of West Bretton – from Sir William Wentworth (died 1763) to the first Viscount Allendale (died 1923).

The present village church, in Huddersfield Road, was opened in 1994. It was a remodelling of the former Methodist Church which had been created in the nineteenth century from a cottage. Unlike most other villages where Methodism became established, no purpose-built chapel was ever erected. Opposition from Establishment-orientated landowners

The centre of West Bretton in the 1930s. The bowed windows of the former village inn may be seen on the far left. Known as the Beaumont's Arms, it was closed down by the landowner in 1897. 'Navvis' constructing a railway tunnel to the east of the village had apparently made too full a use of its facilities.

would have precluded that. In 1982 the Methodist building became the home of the Church in West Bretton – the joining together of Anglicans and Methodists in a partnership, with support and encouragement from the parent denominations.

Other buildings of interest in the village include the school founded by Sir Thomas Blackett of Bretton Hall, who some time before his death in 1792 built a Schoolmaster's house and two classrooms to be used for day and Sunday School purposes. The village's War Memorial was constructed in 1921 with stone taken from the site of an old menagerie in Bretton Park – which accounts for its rather strange shape. Nearby is the bow-windowed house which, until 1897, was the village inn, when it was seemingly closed down by the squire after a period of disturbance caused by 'navvies' then constructing a railway in the vicinity.

The Legend of Bretton Hall

For many years an ancient hat and pair of boots were kept at the Hall. They had reputedly belonged to a member of the Wentworth family who, it was said, had joined a party of scientific explorers determined to discover whether the world was round or flat. When, after many years, he did not return, he was assumed dead and his wife was persuaded to remarry. Fortuitously, he did return – on the day of her wedding. For a while he was unrecognized but then made himself known to his wife. Her wedding to another was called off and the couple lived together at West Bretton, ' happily ever after'.

The story is almost wholly fictitious, and appears to have originated in a poem written by Jimmy Mann – a celebrated local pedlar – in the 1830s. It echoes similar folk stories found in other parts of the country.

At Bretton Hall, near Wakefield, known so well,
Sir William Wentworth Blackett once did dwell;
That mansion was his own; there, with his bride,
In pomp and splendour, he did once reside.
Yet, in the midst of all that he possest,
A rambling mind disturbed Sir William's breast;
His lady and his home he left behind;
Says he, 'The end of this wide world I'll find;

The earth's extensive, but, you may depend on't,
Before e'er I return I'll find the end on't.'
So he embark'd on board a ship, we find,
And, sailing, left her ladyship behind,
Who oft in sorrow did his absence mourn,
And sighing, said, 'Oh, that he would return,
For, be his voyage rough or smooth at sea,
It is a cruel bitter blast to me.'
Sir William, he rolls on through winds and waves,
Undaunted, he all kinds of weather braves;
Nor his strange project e'er relinquished he,
Till one-and-twenty years he'd been at sea;
Then, p'rhaps, he thought, 'Good lack! the world is round;
The end is nowhere – so it can't be found.
And, as I'm weary of this wild goose chase,
At home again ere long I'll show my face.'
Then off he set, but little was aware
What would transpire on his arrival there;
For while Sir William rov'd as here express'd,
Another 'Sir' his lady thus address'd:
'Sir William's gone (ne'er to return again),
Past this world's end which long he sought in vain,
There's not a doubt he's found the end of life;
But don't be troubled – you shall be my wife.'
She listen'd, till at length she gave consent,
And straightway then to church this couple went.
Sir William does about this wedding hear
As he unto his journey's end draws near;
And thus he does within his mind reflect –
'This sly usurper I shall now detect.
Soon shall I know, though much against his will,
At Bretton Hall I have dominion still;
These woods and fertile fields my own I call,
With this magnificent, this splendid hall;
And now I come to claim them as my own,
Though, by my dress, not from a beggar known;
My clothes are turn'd to rags, and by the weather
My skin is tann'd till it resembles leather.
So now I'll act the beggar bold and rude,
And at this wedding boldly I'll intrude,

And though admittance I may be denied,
I'll rob the merry bridegroom of his bride.'
Then at his own hall door one rap he gave
Resolv'd the inmates' charity to crave.
So he present'd his request, 'tis said,
And they presented him – a crust of bread!
The bread he took, and then, to their surprise,
He ask'd the servants for some beer likewise.
'No, no,' said they, 'beer we will give you none,
You saucy, drunken vagabond, begone!'
At length (with much ado) some beer he got,
And quickly he return'd the empty pot;
And straightway then into the hall went he,
And said her ladyship he wish'd to see.
'You can by no means see her,' answer'd they,
'She's newly married! 'Tis her wedding day!'
'Married!' the feigned beggarman replied,
'Then I'll not go till I have seen the bride.'
Then tow'rds the dining-room his course he bent;
The servants quick pursued with one consent,
And seized him, with intent to turn him out.
'Come back, you villain! What are you about?'
'About my business, to be sure,' quoth he;
'The room I'll enter, and the bride I'll see.'
'We'll see you out of doors,' the servants said;
And now, of course, a clam'rous din they made.
Just then the bride, on hearing such a clatter,
Open'd the door, to see what was the matter.
This noble beggar thus obtain'd a sight
Of her who erstwhile was his heart's delight.
He viewed her in her nuptial garments dress'd,
And did of her a glass of wine request,
Which she denied – who little did suppose
The ragged stranger was her wealthy spouse;
Then straight into the dining-room he went,
And down he sat among the guests content.
Says he, 'You'll grant me my request, I know;
A glass of wine I'll have before I go.'
The bride at length complied with his request,
Thus thinking to despatch the ragged guest;

But when he did this glass of wine obtain
He drank and filled, and drank and filled again.
The guests astonish'd and disgusted view'd,
Whilst he proceeded to be far more rude;
Around the bride's fair neck he threw his arm,
And gave a kiss, which did her much alarm.
On him she frown'd, and threaten'd him with law,
Says he, 'Your threats I value not a straw;
My conduct to reprove is all in vain,
For what I've done I mean to do again.
Madam, your bridegroom's in an awkward case;
This night I do intend to take his place.'
And while upon her countenance he pores
The guests agree to kick him out of doors.
'The deuce is in the beggarman,' they cried:
'He means to either beg or steal the bride.'
'No, no,' says he, 'I claim her as my own.'
He smil'd, and then he did himself make known,
Saying, 'William Wentworth Blackett is my name;
For my long absence I'm much to blame;
But safe and sound I have return'd at last,
So let's forgive each other all that's past.'
The bride did her first bridegroom recognise,
With joy transported to his arms she flies;
And, whilst they tenderly each other kiss,
The disappointed bridegroom they dismiss,
Who inwardly did his hard case lament,
Hung down his head, and out of door he went.
'I'm robb'd of this fair jewel now,' thinks he;
'How cruel is this tender spouse to me!'
Awhile he scratched his head, then heav'd a sigh,
Then eyed the hall again, and wip'd his eye.
Sir William freely did forgive his wife:
They liv'd together to the end of life.
My honest story I must now conclude,
Which may by some be as a fiction view'd;
But, Sirs, the boots in which Sir William went
Are kept in memory of that event;
The very hat he wore preserved has been
At Bretton Hall – where they may yet be seen.

The George and Dragon Inn, situated at the eastern end of the village of Flockton, is a fine, partly timbered building, which provides an unexpected sight in a village dominated by

Flockton

SPRAWLED ALONG THE FORMER BARNSLEY-GRANGE MOOR TURNPIKE, on the hillside rising to Flockton Moor – where one of the Dearne tributaries rises – the ancient hamlets of Over and Nether Flockton have long since merged into one village. Settlements where landownership was divided, the medieval communities were once dominated by such long-forgotten families as the de Birkins, de Flocktons and de Horburys. By the thirteenth century the de Wortleys, ancestors of the Earls of Wharncliffe of Wortley near Penistone, had gained a significant holding in the district. It was a holding which was eventually to pass to the Beaumont family of Bretton Hall. After the Reformation, the Kayes (later Lister-Kayes) had become the owners of the nearby Denby Grange Estate which had formerly been a centre for monastic agricultural and industrial activities in the locality.

The presence of substantial reserves of iron ore and coal was to be a vital factor in the community's survival – resources which were exploited for centuries. Indeed, the village has given its name to the Flockton Thick and Flockton Thin seams of the Yorkshire Coalfield. Monks from the North Yorkshire abbeys of Byland and Rievaulx were being granted pasture and mining rights in the area as early as the twelfth century, and large-scale coal mining was to become a very important feature in village life during the eighteenth and nineteenth centuries. Many relics of that worked-out industry may be found on both the west and east sides of the village. The countryside to the south-east of the village, surrounding the site of the medieval New Hall, is an industrial archeologist's dream – with remains of wagonways, tunnels, shafts and spoil heaps.

One such site lies beside the A637 between Flockton and the hamlet of Midgley at Lane End. Closed at the end of the nineteenth century, the colliery was one of several within the industrial empire of the Milnes-Stansfeld family. Moving on from their background of

The remains of a waggonway by which coal was conveyed from the former Lane End Colliery at Flockton to the Calder and Hebble Navigation at Horbury Bridge.

The former Caphouse Colliery – now the National Mining Museum of England.

farming, malt-making and dealing in timber, they became influential people in Flockton and injected a great deal of vigour into the economic and social life of the community. At one time they were employing some 500 men and boys, and encouraging various social and educational activities in the village. Government Commissioners, collecting evidence for a report on the state of the population in mining areas, visited Flockton in the 1840s and felt moved to comment on its substantial dwellings, considerable educational resources, strong horticultural and temperance societies, and generous sporting facilities. They might also have noted the thriving 'Flockton United Band', founded in 1838; or, if they had visited the village some thirty years later, the formation of a Co-operative Society.

Unfortunately for the Milnes-Stansfeld family, constraints were increasingly placed on the further development of their industry by lack of access to a railway system. A wooden wagonway leading to the Calder and Hebble Canal at Horbury Bridge (traces of which may still be seen) proved to be less and less satisfactory. Their empire gradually

The Parish Church of St James the Great in Flockton, consecrated in 1869. In the foreground stands the building of the former Flockton Grammar School founded by Richard Carter in 1699.

declined. In spite of many efforts to save it, Lane End Colliery did not re-open after a sixteen-week strike by miners in 1893. The street name, Manor Drive, is now the only reminder of their manor house in which they lived until the end of the nineteenth century.

That was not to be the end of coal mining in Flockton, however, for lying outside the Dearne Valley though intrinsically bound up with Flockton life are the many remains of the Lister-Kaye involvement in the industry, including Caphouse Colliery – now the National Mining Museum of England. That this enterprise did not follow in the path of the Milnes-Stansfeld decline is due to the fact that it did have a railway link. Following the pertinent and informed advice given to the family by a Wakefield lawyer, John Marsden (who was much experienced in the management of landed estates with coal resources), a branch line was built to Calder Grove, in the 1850s, at a cost of some £30,000. His advice paid off to such an extent that he has been called, by one distinguished local historian, 'the Father of the Denby Grange Collieries'.

Amongst the more noteworthy buildings in the village is the Parish Church of St James the Great. The present building and burial ground were consecrated by the Bishop of Ripon on 1st September 1869. It replaced a seventeenth century building situated in the old graveyard on the opposite side of the road, which had been described by one observer as 'an old incommodious edifice'. The simple, unpretentious building, with a stone exterior and interior of yellow bricks and red arches, was built under the direction of a committee which had to proceed under some considerable economic restrictions. The Church authorities accepted that a new building was necessary, but the diocese (then the Diocese of Ripon) had been able to make a grant of only £150, and the highest personal subscription to the appeal had been no more than £100. As much help as possible had therefore to be sought from local working people and, even then, when the Church was consecrated, there was still a debt of almost £700. That the church was completed at all must have given considerable satisfaction to those who were most closely involved. A writer in the Wakefield Journal and Examiner of 17th September 1869, describing the consecration, poignantly commented:

> The villagers, several of whom had given voluntary labour in the work, took very great interest in the proceedings. Every face wore an expression of grave gladness...

Until 1860, Flockton had been a chapelry within the ancient parish of Thornhill. A growing population had made that arrangement increasingly unsatisfactory. An independent parish with a new worship centre, it was hoped, could enable the Established Church to come to terms more effectively with the working people of an industrial village.

Where once there were several nonconformist chapels in the village, now there is only one – the Zion United Reformed Church. On the western extremity of the village, standing back from the road and surrounded by an extensive graveyard, the Church was opened as a preaching place for a society of 'Independents' in 1802. Most of the impetus for its building came from a Mr John Bond, a London resident and a successful merchant trading in the West Indies. Having come into possession of property in Flockton, and being of 'Independent' persuasion, he helped to provide a chapel that did away with a need to worship in private houses.

The exterior of the building is plain and functional – a typical nonconformist chapel of that era. This is generally echoed inside, though the chief feature is a superb double-decker pulpit. Its history has unfortunately not been discovered, but it may be older than the

Zion United Reformed Church in Flockton: the exterior and graveyard.

The interior of the church with its double decker pulpit. It has been suggested that the pulpit may be older than the church building and that a precentor used the lower deck and the minister the upper one where he could be seen by all members of the congregation.

building itself.

Many nonconformist societies, in their early days, had to balance their budgets very carefully and, if they were able to 'call' a full-time preacher to lead their activities, then he was usually forced to live very frugally. The minister of this church in the 1830s was the Revd John Sowerby. For two years the church was only able to pay him an annual stipend of £8 and, for several subsequent years, varying amounts of which the highest was £20. Since he was a weaver by trade, he was able to supplement his income by working at his loom. It was said that 'while he manufactured cloth he also manufactured sermons for his flock on the Lord's Day'.

Structured education has been a feature of Flockton life since the seventeenth century, when a Grammar School was endowed for the teaching of Latin and Greek to selected boys. In 1699 Richard Carter, a local industrialist and benefactor, made financial provision for six poor boys to be taught in this school. The venture continued into the nineteenth century when a reorganisation of what had become a fairly moribund institution resulted in the building of a new school. This was strongly supported by members of the Lister-Kaye family, and was intended to provide weekday, night school and Sunday School facilities. From this developed the present village primary school. Stones bearing dates and initials have been set into the wall of the present building, and serve as a reminder of three centuries of educational provision.

Within Flockton's mixture of council housing estates, commuter dwellings and older cottages, interspersed with roads bearing personal names such as Hardcastle or Haigh, or names like Pinfold Lane that bring to mind the occupations of a rural society, are two other prominent buildings – one ancient, the other modern. At the eastern end of the village is the George and Dragon Inn, a fine timbered building which provides a delightfully unexpected sight in a village so dominated by brickwork and stone. Reputed to be one of the oldest licensed houses in the vicinity, parts of it are said to date back to about 1485. Drinking tastes are also catered for, about half a mile to the west, in the Working Men's Club, a large twentieth century building – less pleasing aesthetically, but no doubt providing an equally-welcome service.

Two former Flockton buildings

Flockton Hall, formerly the home of the Rhodes family – another local family who 'made good'. It was demolished in the 1950s as a consequence of damage caused by mining subsidence.

According to the Census Returns of 1861 Flockton had eleven public houses. Most have since disappeared, including the **Angel Inn** – now a private residence.

Emley

AN HISTORICAL SETTLEMENT to which some industry was drawn in medieval times and later, with the exception of coal mining, almost wholly left, the village contains numerous features which provide insight into life in previous centuries.

Untouched by turnpike roads, canals or railways, the village was for several centuries one of the homes of a branch of the Fitzwilliam family whose seats were at Emley Hall and Sprotborough near Doncaster. In 1516, ownership passed by marriage into the hands of the Saviles – a prominent Yorkshire gentry family who lived at (the now ruined) Thornhill Hall near Dewsbury. During the turmoils of the English Civil War, the Saviles found their sympathies lying with the Royalist cause and, as a consequence of the triumph of the Puritans, were forced to surrender their home. Moving to another of their estates at Rufford Abbey in Nottinghamshire, their descendants retained the ownership of much of Emley, as they still do. The present 'lordship' is held by the third Baron Savile, who lives at Gryce Hall in the nearby village of Shelley, having moved from Rufford in 1938.

The outstanding building in the village, and for many miles around, is the Parish Church of St. Michael. The greater part of the building dates from the fifteenth century and contains fragments of earlier eras including Anglo-Saxon grave slabs and a Norman tympanum – set into the interior wall, near to the pulpit. One of the church's particularly charming features, unique to this district, is the nave roof with its rough beams and king posts.

As is the case with so many other ancient parish churches throughout the country, numerous alterations have been carried out at various times. The Kirkby (or Assheton) chapel was added in 1632; the tulip shaped font probably about the same time; and the splendid brass candelabra in the chancel was installed in 1832. A thorough restoration of the whole building took place in the 1870s (a decade of many such restorations), which included the provision of the present pews, choir

The house at Emley Old Hall Farm. Built on the former site of the residence of the Fitzwilliam family, it has been described as the 'most historic site in Emley'. Remains of the moat can still be seen around the farmstead.

The Parish Church of St Michael, Emley

The remains of a Norman tympanum built into an interior wall in Emley Church.

stalls and chancel screen.

A facsimile of the Royal Charter of 1253 authorising the right for markets and fairs to be held in the village may be seen in the church, and a fine collection of parish records of many kinds, formerly kept in the church, is now preserved in the West Yorkshire County Archive office in Wakefield.

The people of Emley, proud of their heritage, have preserved several other remains of their past – which are now set into the churchyard wall, near the War Memorial. Here is the doorway of a former seventeenth century school building that once stood on this site. Founded and endowed by one John Wiglesworth in 1673, it ceased to function in the early years of the nineteenth century and was dismantled in 1847. Nearby, a stone cross bearing the date 1683 was removed from a former cottage in the village. It appears to be the symbol of the Knights of St John of Jerusalem who owned property in the village prior to the Reformation. Also nearby is a curious and blunt inscription:

If fortune keep thee warm
Thy friends about thee swarm
Like bees about a hony pot
But if she frown and cast thee down
Lye there and rott.

On the opposite side of the road from the parish church is the parish hall built in 1872 as an infants' school and run in association with the National Society. It had been intended, by the Rector of the parish at that time, that it would be followed by a junior department, and so counteract the influence of the village's British School, but the plan never reached fruition. Indeed in 1928 the infants were actually moved to the former British School, by then run by the West Riding County Council. The building became the parish hall in 1933.

Opened in 1852, the British School was the only such institution in the village to have links with the interdenominational British and Foreign Society. Its foundation owed a great deal to the Revd Robert Pym, incumbent of the parish from 1830-62. Pym seems to have been quite a remarkable man, who was increasingly drawn to Calvinistic belief and whose preaching drew considerable support from surrounding villages. He felt able to join with nonconformists in a way that neither his predecessor nor successor felt able to do. Indeed he actually gave active support to the building of a Baptist chapel in

The former doorway of the seventeenth century school in Emley, endowed by John Wiglesworth in 1673.

Clayton West in the1840s. It was intended that Emley British School should cater for children of all religious backgrounds, and its foundation deed stressed that:

> No catechism or other formulary peculiar to any religious denomination shall be introduced or taught.

A badly-corroded stone set into the wall of the building records that the school was built on land 'kindly and liberally given by Thomas Wentworth Beaumont of Bretton Hall.' The original foundation was vested in a body of trustees but, in 1902, it came under the jurisdiction of the West Riding County Council and has remained as a local authority school ever since.

The neat Methodist chapel, situated in Church Street a few metres from the Parish Hall, was erected in 1912 for a society of Primitive Methodists and replaced an older building of 1850. That building had in turn replaced a preaching-place of 1828 which, after a turbulent argument, had been lost by the society. The mid-nineteenth century seems to have been a very unsettled time for many nonconformist groups. Arguments over organisation and purity of belief led to numerous secessions, not least in Emley. A dissenting group who called themselves Free Methodists appropriated the 1828 chapel, and the Primitive Methodists were forced to reorganise themselves.

Before the Primitive Methodists had appeared on the scene, Emley had been a centre for Wesleyan Methodist activities. In 1766. in spite of the efforts of the then Rector, the Revd John Woollin, to frustrate their work, the village had become one of the first places in the valley in which the followers of John Wesley had gained a foothold. In 1798 a room in a cottage was licensed for their preaching, and a chapel followed in 1811. By the 1870s the society was struggling, and its chapel finally closed in 1913. The building in Warburton remains as a private residence.

It has already been noted that Emley became a place of considerable commercial and industrial importance in medieval times, and that a weekly market and annual fair were authorised from 1253. The site of the markets and fairs is to be found in the centre of the village, together with a white-washed remnant of the market cross. Village tradition records that here, in 1826, one John Turton sold his wife for two half-crowns to a William Kaye of Scissett. This was, of course, an illegal act, but not an unknown procedure in an era when divorce was only

The remains of Emley Market Cross (above); and (below) the Cross overlooked by the former Reading Room, Blacksmith's shop and Temperance Hotel.

obtainable by a personal Act of Parliament and therefore limited to the rich and influential.

Surrounding the square are miscellaneous buildings which, with the passage of time, have changed their function: the former Emley Co-operative store, the Temperance Hotel, the Blacksmith's shop, the Reading Room of 1879 (an important educational facility in Victorian times, containing both a library and a collection of daily newspapers), and the Post Office. Emley Moor, the exposed and now enclosed former common land of the parish, has in the late twentieth century become the site of arguably the most striking landmark in West Yorkshire and Europe's tallest free-standing structure – the 300 metre television mast. The concrete tower, visible for many miles around, was constructed in 1970 following the collapse of an earlier metal mast in March 1969. In a fierce winter onslaught the weight of ice on its guy-ropes brought about its destruction, and much damage was caused to surrounding buildings, especially the former Methodist chapel. No lives were lost, but two people who were inside the chapel at the time – investigating leaks in the roof – had a very narrow escape.

In the outlying parts of the parish are several noteworthy houses. Lying between the villages of Emley and Flockton, and occupying a site that has been inhabited for at least a thousand years, is Kirkby Grange. The house, which is now divided into apartments, is an architectural treasure with its prominent gables and mullioned windows – produced in an age when techniques for manufacturing large panes of glass had not been perfected. It was built about 1607 for Ralph Assheton, a member of a prominent Lancastrian family and one of the forbears of the Lords Clitheroe of Downham. The Assheton Chapel in St Michael's Church, as well as this house, remains as a memorial to a family that was prominent in Emley life for about a century. Towards the end of the seventeenth century, when the Asshetons left the district, the property came into the hands of a family called Wheelwright. In 1724, with the death of John Wheelwright, it was sold again and part of the proceeds were used, under the terms of John's will, to endow the Wheelwright Grammar School in Dewsbury.

The early seventeenth century seems to have been a time of substantial building and rebuilding in the village. In 1623, only sixteen years after the Asshetons had built Kirkby Grange, members of another prominent local family, the Allots, were building Thorncliffe Grange on the south-eastern side of the village. This gabled house, with transomed windows and very sturdy walls (over two feet thick in places)

A stone cross bearing the date 1683, set into the churchyard wall in Emley. Removed from a former cottage, it appears to be the symbol of the Knights of St John of Jerusalem, who may have owned property in the village prior to the Reformation.

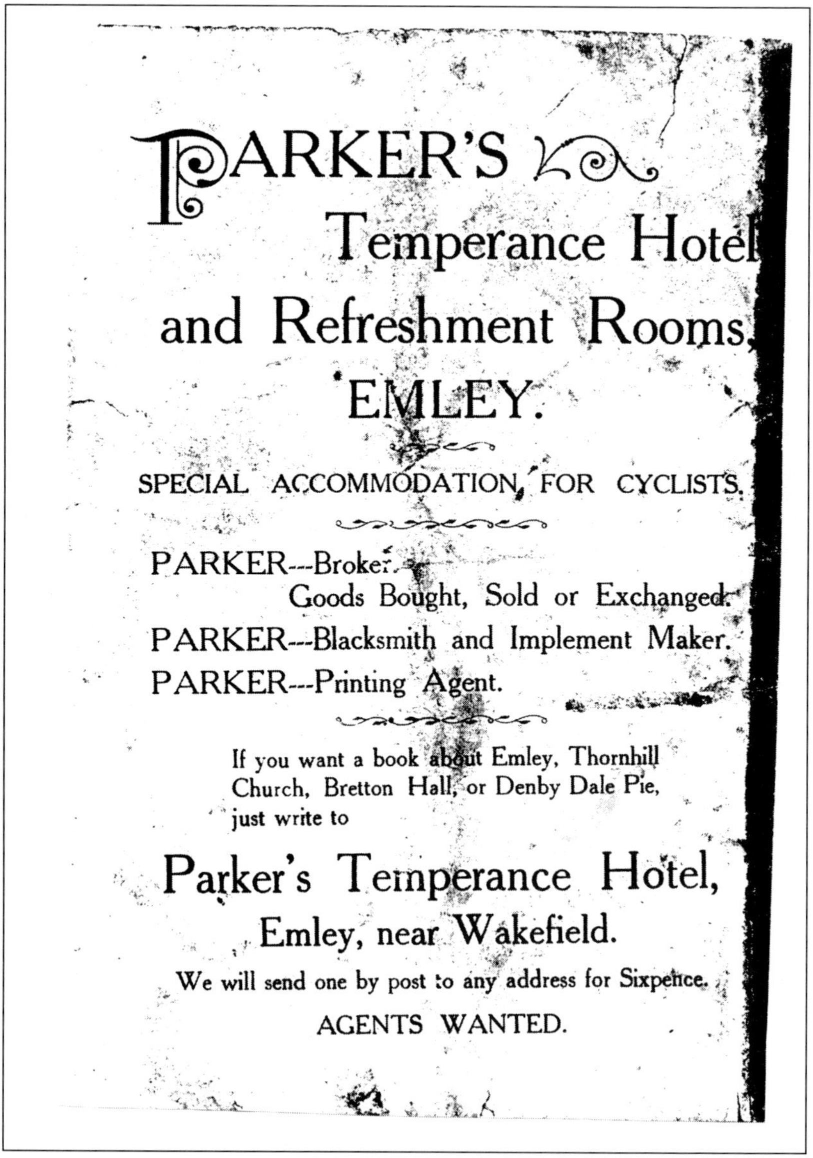

The Temperance Movement originated in England in the 1820s as a voluntary attempt to do something about the grave social problems that were caused by alcohol abuse. It found expression in the foundation of such groups as the Band of Hope and, as here in Emley, in attempts to provide an alternative to the public house. A similar facility was also provided in Cawthorne.

The former Wesleyan Reform chapel in Emley. Opened in July 1854, it has recently been demolished, to be replaced by dwelling houses.

witnessed pillaging by Parliamentary troops during the Civil War.

About a mile to the south of the village is Emley Woodhouse, a graceful Georgian building occupying a site that is mentioned in legal documents reaching back into the thirteenth century. In the valley below, on the road that leads to West Bretton, is Bentley Grange. Surrounded by the numerous grass-covered mounds that are the remains of iron-ore mine spoil-heaps, the Grange now betrays only a few signs of its former importance. For long the centre of the agricultural and industrial activities of medieval monks from the North Yorkshire Abbey of Byland, the present buildings date mainly from the eighteenth century, though incorporating stones and timbers from earlier constructions.

For almost four hundred years the Grange was the home of the chief branch of the Allot family of Emley, who maybe provide an illustration of the truth to be found in the proverbial saying: 'From clogs to clogs in three generations' – though perhaps not, in this case, in just three generations. The Allots lived first at Bentley as tenant ironmasters of Byland, for after the devastation of the Black Death, the monks did not have sufficient manpower to continue the workings themselves. With the Dissolution of the Monasteries, the family carefully contrived to come into possession of the property and retained it until 1707. Thereafter, having passed the peak of their prosperity, arrangements were made for Bentley to be purchased by the Wentworths of the nearby Bretton Hall. And thus the Allots became tenants again. Numerous inscribed stones, both at the Grange and within the Parish Church – together with remaining documents – make it clear that this was an important family in village life for many years.

Near to the site of the former Park Mill Colliery, between Emley and Clayton West, is the site of the former Emley Hall, seat of the Fitzwilliams. Eighteenth century buildings of no particular distinction occupy a site that has been called the most historic in Emley. The visible remains of a moat indicate a possible pre-Norman habitation. Indeed, it might be said that, on this spot, the first settlement of Emley took root.

Two particular aspects of present-day village life deserve special mention: the agricultural show and the football club. The show began in 1877 as a village flower show. Over the years it has developed into one of the largest agricultural shows in the district. Sited near to the

Part of the 300 metre Emley Moor television mast which collapsed under the weight of ice in March 1969, causing much damage to the nearby Methodist chapel. The top of the mast, which was then the tallest structure in Europe, landed a third of a mile from the base.

Building work is begun on the present concrete tower.

The present 300 metre television mast at Emley Moor, constructed in 1970. Signals from the concrete tower are transmitted within a vast area, reaching to the Scottish border in the north and Oxfordshire in the south.

Two Emley Houses

Kirkby Grange – built in 1607 for Ralph Assheton. It is now divided into apartments and the outbuildings have been converted into dwellings.

Emley Woodhouse – a graceful Georgian dwelling occupying a site which is mentioned in legal documents from the thirteenth century.

Dearne, alongside the Wakefield-Denby Dale road, it provides entertainment and education in rural pursuits for thousands of people on the first Saturday in August each year. The football club was founded in 1904 and has also moved on from small beginnings, attracting fame and acclamation in the process. In 1973 the club entered the preliminary rounds of the F.A. Cup for the first time, though it was to be 1991 before it managed to reach the first round proper. But it was in 1998 that the Club achieved what many thought was the impossible by reaching the third round of the competition. Drawn against the mighty West Ham United, Emley actually managed to dominate in much of the play, and came within nine minutes of forcing a replay. Defeat by two goals to one was a sign of triumph for the team, whose shirts bore the logo: 'By 'eck who's Emley'.

E. Cudworth

"Old Emley"

FOLK SONG.

Words by
G. SELWYN BALL.

Music by
J. W. WALKER (Nelson).

(Dedicated to the Memory of the late John Thorp and Others).

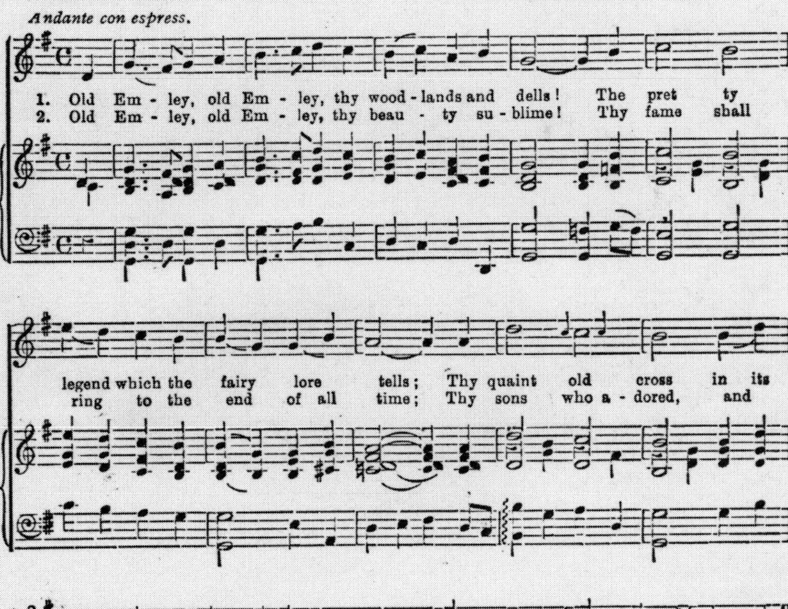

[3d.] Published by G. SELWYN BALL, 12, Lomeshaye Rd., Nelson, Lancs.

A curious relic of Emley's history – though whether it still exists has not been discovered by the author.

The interior of the Parish Church of St Michael the Archangel, in Emley

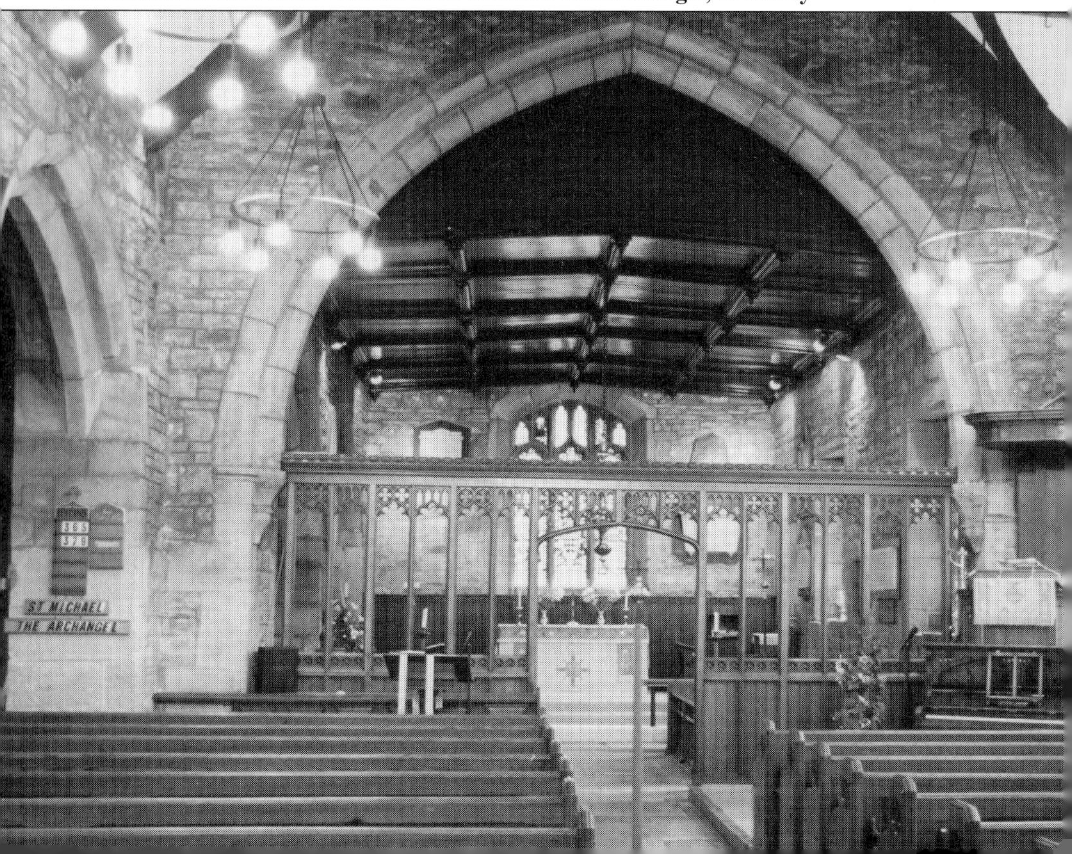

Clayton West

THE VISITOR TO CLAYTON WEST TODAY finds a substantial urban community, much of which is little older than the nineteenth century, to which considerable twentieth century additions have been made. What was once a small agricultural settlement within the parish of High Hoyland was to be transformed by the Industrial Revolution. Left out on a limb is the historic Clayton Hall, now an isolated farmstead on the hillside between the village and Bretton Park. Here and there, within the modern village, traces of older farmsteads and cottages may be seen.

In the eighteenth century a number of spinners, weavers and small clothiers were settled in the vicinity, utilising the water of the river Dearne, and a new kind of settlement developed which grew steadily and constantly in size and prosperity. By 1837 the village had a population of 887, and contained worsted and silk mills. Ten years later the population had more than doubled. Expansion continued until the First World War, boosted by the opening of the Wakefield to Denby Dale turnpike road in 1842 and the construction of a branch line to connect with the Huddersfield-Penistone railway in 1875. In fact the village came very near to being the place where Sir Titus Salt might have built his alpaca mill. He investigated a particular site with interest, but that land was to be intersected by the railway and Sir Titus therefore turned his attention to the Bradford area and went on to develop Saltaire. Since the 1920s the village has lost much of its industry, and become a commuter settlement.

One of the historic delights in the village is the old packhorse bridge – just off the Wakefield-Denby Dale road, near to the Woodman Inn. Built in the sixteenth century, it formerly carried the highway from the village to Emley and West Bretton, and thence to Wakefield. The construction of the turnpike rendered it superfluous.

In 1764, the Rector of High Hoyland informed Archbishop Drummond of York that, within the parish:

> Some interlopers from places infected with Methodism are endeavouring to propagate their notions, but gain few proselytes. There is no licensed or other meeting house, except

> a few private houses maybe called so, where the above crazy visionaries sometimes assemble.

A century later, the situation had been completely transformed. A visitor to the village in the 1870s commented on the great variety of the religious buildings that he had found: Episcopalians, Independents, Baptists, Wesleyans, New Connexion Methodists and Primitive Methodists. Times have changed again, and the numerous places of worship that were then found have been reduced. The village provided, until quite recently, a classic illustration of the growth of nonconformity in a situation where the Church of England had become increasingly ineffectual.

Standing starkly, indeed almost precariously, on the hillside is the United Reformed Church opened in 1866, replacing an earlier chapel of 1794. The Independents (later to be known as Congregationalists and, more recently, on amalgamating with Presbyterians, to create the United Reformed Church) were the first nonconformist group in the village, and were active for some years before building a chapel. In the

The Woodman Inn at Clayton West, as it appeared in the early twentieth century. In the background may be seen the packhorse bridge which formerly carried the road from Clayton West to Emley.

A closer view of the **packhorse bridge**.

1820s the Baptists appeared on the scene, and their building in High Street, which is no longer in use for religious purposes, was opened in 1840. Active support to its foundation was given by the Revd Robert Pym, the somewhat unorthodox and puritanically-inclined Rector of Emley of that era. In 1857 the Primitive Methodists built their chapel

The former **Baptist Chapel** in Clayton West - opened in 1840.

near to the turnpike road to serve both Clayton West and Scissett, and that building survives as the only Methodist chapel in the village. Two others have been demolished, as has a former Wesleyan Reform chapel. Much more recently, a Pentecostal Church has been opened.

The Parish Church of All Saints was consecrated by the Bishop of Ripon in 1875. It was built at a cost of almost £2,300 when it was decided that the Church in High Hoyland could no longer be used as an effective Anglican centre for the whole parish. However, the Rector continued to be known as the Rector of High Hoyland with Clayton

The Parish Church of All Saints in Clayton West - consecrated in 1875.

West and, since no burial ground was attached to the new building, interments continued to take place at High Hoyland. The building of the new church was done against a background of considerable opposition from the nonconformists of the area, who seem to have regarded the village as their own special territory. An article published in the *Barnsley Chronicle* shortly after the consecration stated:

> The Church has been erected under very great difficulties. The Dissenters of the neighbourhood were ruthless in their opposition.

That the liturgical practices of the new church reflected nineteenth

The lodge standing beside a gate that leads into grounds owned and occupied by John Kaye, the 'uncrowned king of Clayton West', in the ninteenth century.

century 'High Church' ideals probably fuelled the opposition, as it did in various other parts of the country when it was thought that 'Popery' was being re-introduced into a Protestant country.

Within the Parish Church is a memorial to Captain C.J. Wintour, son of the Revd Fitzgerald Wintour – the Rector of High Hoyland who was largely responsible for the building being established. Captain Wintour was killed at the Battle of Jutland in 1916, when commanding a flotilla of destroyers.

Prominent in village life in the Victorian era was John Kaye, textile manufacturer and the so-called uncrowned 'King of Clayton West'. Park House, formerly his residence, no longer remains, though part of its surrounding parkland and one of the lodges does. His name survives, however, in the village school. A National School had been founded in 1816, sited between High Hoyland and Clayton West to cater for the needs of children in both villages. The strong-willed Kaye, however, found himself in disagreement with the parish Rector on educational matters. Being a man of substance, as well as determination, he decided to build another school in which he could exercise his influence. In the heart of the village, that school building was extended in the 1870s and became a 'Board School' – though carefully preserving, as it still does, the name of 'Kaye'.

The days of Clayton West as the active terminus of a branch line linked to the former Huddersfield-Penistone railway ended in January 1983. Left behind were rusty lines, a rather forlorn-looking station, and a signal box – as reminders of the important ways in which local industry and rail transport had once been intertwined. Little did anyone realise at the time that there would in fact be a 'resurrection' of rail travel, albeit on a rather different scale. In 1991 the Kirklees Light Railway opened as a tourist attraction. It operates on a 15 inch gauge line, laid on the track bed of the original railway. A small staff and a number of volunteers provide a service which may be a far cry from what was once there, but which offers interest and pleasure to people in the district.

The former railway station at Clayton West, closed in 1983

Scissett

IN 1980 THE RESIDENTS OF SCISSETT celebrated what they considered to be the community's 150th birthday. Before 1830, the village was largely undeveloped – an area of wooded countryside on the north bank of the river, lying within the township of Skelmanthorpe and the parish of High Hoyland. Then, in 1825, as has been seen, Joseph Norton (a local clothier) purchased Highbridge Corn Mill with an adjacent piece of land and founded, not only Nortonthorpe Mills, but also the village. From a modest beginning an industrial enterprise grew until it was providing employment for a thousand people. The village grew fairly constantly until about 1870, with shops, three public houses and numerous tradespeople. It also, for a time, boasted a market – long since gone.

From time to time the business was forced to adapt as fashions changed or as the economic situation varied. A thriving involvement in the 'fancy' trade gave way, in the early years of the twentieth

Nortonthorpe Mills at Scissett - a village which owes its existence to the development of the textile industry.

century, to fabric weaving. But, by 1985, the business was no more. In that year the buildings (now in new ownership) were converted into the Nortonthorpe Industrial Park, housing offices, shops and industrial units. Today the Norton buildings have been given a new lease of life and are surrounded by shops, commuter dwellings, and the premises of other businesses – including a printing works.

Standing outside the front entrance to the mill complex, near to the large pond, it does not need a great deal of imagination to relive the events of 1842. It was in August of that year that a large band of disaffected textile workers from Lancashire and Yorkshire, fearing for their jobs in the face of increasing mechanisation, marched on Nortonthorpe Mills intending to stop production by drawing out the boiler plugs. Their demonstration was to be fruitless. An alert cavalry had been forewarned and was ready and prepared. The Riot Act was read. Warnings were given of the dire possibility of transportation for any who broke the law. The crowds gradually dispersed.

A unique part of the mill's history is of particular interest to steam enthusiasts. A rare 'Pollit and Wigzell' steam engine reclines gracefully in the engine house. In the mill's earliest days, the river itself was the source of power. Two water-wheels harnessed the power that ran the machinery. At a later stage a steam-powered beam engine was installed to supplement that supply. Popularly known as 'Ben', the beam engine was replaced in 1886 by the present machine. At first it was given the name 'Empress' in honour of Queen Victoria, who was then Empress of India, but its name was changed following an overhaul in 1906. The overhaul coincided with the birth of a daughter to George Norton, the mill owner. He named his daughter Violet and, in celebration, the steam engine was given the same name. With careful attention, 'Violet' worked regularly until 1962. Then, with the full electrification of the mill, she was granted a well-earned retirement. Eleven years later, when severe power cuts occurred, she was brought back into temporary use. From time to time 'Violet' may be seen by the public, steaming happily, having been lovingly restored to her former glory.

On the slopes to the north and west of the village stand Nortonthorpe Hall (built by Joseph Norton) and Bagden Hall (built by his brother George). Both are typical mill-owners' houses of the Victorian era and both are a visible commentary on the prosperity which came to the family, together with a consequent rise in their station in life. But, in the fashion of many a Yorkshire mill owner, neither wished to be too

Bagden Hall Hotel – formerly the home of George Norton

far away from 'the shop'. Their gentlemanly spaciousness and privacy was so ordered that they could keep a careful eye on the source of their wealth. Today, Nortonthorpe Hall is used for educational purposes, whilst Bagden Hall has been converted into a high quality hotel.

Within the village, the parish church of St. Augustine was consecrated in 1839 to cater for the increasing population of the district. An apsed chancel was added in 1881. The building, with its lancet windows, has no great architectural distinction but, internally, it possesses an interesting wrought-iron rood-screen separating nave from chancel.

The former National School of the nineteenth century is now disused. The Victorian building, with its high gables and windows, is a typical school building of the late nineteenth century . A new school has been opened on the main Wakefield Road, and its modern design is a complete contrast to that of its predecessor. To compare the two buildings is to learn a great deal about the many changes that have occurred in education during the past century.

South of the village, on the heights which separate the valley from one

St Augustine's Church at Scissett – consecrated in 1839. The apsed chancel was added in 1881.

of its tributaries, are found several farm houses and accompanying outbuildings which are far older than the village itself. Perhaps the most picturesque is Wheatley Hill Farm. The house appears to have been built and remodelled on numerous occasions, from the Elizabethan era onwards, whilst occupying a site which features in legal documents dating from the thirteenth century. A fine timber-framed wing, and a stone gable with mullioned windows, are connected by a strangely modernised frontage. Capping the whole is an enormous chimney which appears almost out of proportion to the rest of the building. Inside the house, an original carved door headstone has been preserved bearing the date 1651 and the name of Peter Hawksworth. The Hawksworth family seem to have lived here for just over a hundred years lapping the sixteenth and seventeenth centuries. A "Peter Hawcksworthe", then a churchwarden at High Hoyland Church, is mentioned as one of the militia mustering at Barnsley on 4th December 1587 in anticipation of the coming of the Spanish Armada. In 1689 Wheatley Hill was sold to John Rhodes of Flockton; in 1710 it became the property of the Spencer-Stanhope family of Cawthorne; in 1916 it was purchased by Thomas Norton of Bagden Hall; and in 1950 it was sold to the sitting tenants.

Wheatley Hill Farm near Scissett. The house appears to have been built and remodelled numerous times. The site is referred to in legal documents dating from the thirteenth century.

A headstone inside Wheatley Hill farmhouse preserves the name of the Hawksworth family who lived here in the sixteenth and seventeenth centuries.

The end wall of a cottage in Skelmanthorpe reveals many signs of adaptation at various times. Most significantly it can be seen that at some stage the roof has been raised – presumably to enable a larger loom to be placed in the upper chamber.

Skelmanthorpe

THE LARGEST COMMUNITY IN THE VALLEY, Skelmanthorpe is, like so many others in the neighbourhood, an industrial village which began life as an agricultural settlement and expanded in the eighteenth and nineteenth centuries. A large number of former clothiers' cottages of that period may be seen; they show how widespread the weaving of woollen cloth had then become. One such cottage, in Queen Street, has been lovingly restored and furnished as it would have been in 1918. Upstairs in 'the chamber' a loom stands close to the mullioned windows just as it would have done many years ago. To walk down the hill from the Huddersfield Road is to enter a labyrinth of narrow winding roads with cottages, terraces and outhouses arranged in a pleasingly unsystematic way and rightly designated as a conservation area. Here and there a former farmstead or barn has been swallowed up in the urban sprawl. One village historian, writing in the late nineteenth century, recalled the Skelmanthorpe of some eighty years earlier as being a manufacturing village in which:

> every farmhouse and every cottage had some kind of rude machinery or contrivance for the manufacture of woollen cloth.

The very observant visitor will discover marks on the gable ends of some of the cottages which show that, at some stage, the roof has had to be heightened so that larger looms might be accomodated on the upper floor.

On 9th May 1757 John Wesley, the founder of Methodism, recorded in his journal:

> I rode over the mountains to Huddersfield. A wilder people I never saw in England. The men, women and children filled the street as we rode along, and appeared just ready to devour us. They were, however, tolerably quiet while I preached; only a few pieces of dirt were thrown .....

Since he had travelled over the Pennines from Lancashire, it is highly unlikely that Wesley visited Skelmanthorpe and formed similar impressions of the residents, but such a roughness in attitude during the late eighteenth and early nineteenth centuries has been noted by several local historians in compiling their studies of a number of villages in the Huddersfield area – including Skelmanthorpe. Prior to the development of better communications, of more educational opportunity, of structured local government, and of greater health care, brutal living conditions – a consequence of the Industrial Revolution – bred brutal behaviour.

Fighting between gangs from villages in the district appears to have been fairly commonplace. Mary Jagger, in writing a history of Honley (a village some four miles from Skelmanthorpe) referred to Skelmanthorpe in the 1820s as being:

> a village in which it was said that a whole man did not exist at that time, having lost fingers, ears and noses .....

as a result of local warfare. Fred Lawton, compiling historical notes from various sources, produced a description of Skelmanthorpe Feast of about the same time:

> The village green ..... was a scene of wild confusion. The public houses were crowded with drunken revellers, who caroused all day and made night hideous with their quarrels and disturbances. A stout stake was fixed in the middle of the green for bull baiting and bear baiting. Here some unhappy bear was chained with only liberty to move around the pole and sit on his hind legs. Savage bull dogs were incited to attack him, and as they pinned him by the nose, and made him yell with pain, the excited crowd screamed with delight .....

The account continued:

> Often two powerful young men would strip and enter the ring for a brutal prize fight, or a match of wrestling. Among these scenes of revelry would be mountebanks, showmen, fortune-telling gypsies, vagabonds, and thieves from every quarter. The din, uproar and strife lasted day and night .....

A final observation was made (possibly with tongue slightly in cheek!):

> work was entirely suspended for a week and the savings of a whole year would be spent in folly and sin.

Perhaps it is hardly surprising that, when the Wesleyan Methodist Church was opened in the village in 1816, John Wood of Denby Dale wrote to the Revd Isaac Clayton:

> We have got a good and very handsome chapel ... I hope it will be a blessing to the inhabitants of that place, for many of them want both civilising and humanising ....

Yet another example of rough behaviour occurred in 1874 when a fight broke out between local inhabitants and Irish 'navvies' who were then building the railway. A series of skirmishes resulted in those Skelmanthorpe men who were also working on the line being turned away. 'Skelmanthorpers' were so incensed by what had happened that a group of them went down to the railway and began throwing stones at the 'foreigners'. The 'navvies' struck back with mattocks and spades and, within a short time, about two hundred men, women and children were caught up in the brawl – the women lending support by filling their aprons with stones for the men to throw. The unrest appears to have lasted for the best part of a day and was only quelled with the arrival of the local constable. He was later joined by reinforcements from Huddersfield.

It would be quite unfair, however, to suggest that such examples of brutal behaviour were typical and constant throughout the nineteenth century. That was not the case and, indeed, there is considerable evidence to show that there was, within the community, a strong desire to bring about an improved quality of life for working people – and not just in the immediate district. The support that Skelmanthorpe people gave to nonconformity, to Chartism and to radical political commitment generally, was all geared to bringing about positive humanitarian change. An earnest people lent support to earnest causes. Moreover a Mechanics' Institute, a Mutual Improvement Society and a Naturalists' Society were once lively features of village life, and the Skelmanthorpe Band, established in the 1850s, still flourishes.

Two of the village's oldest buildings are to be found on the north side of Huddersfield Road. 'Gill Gate', a dark stone residence with mullioned windows, dates from 1642. In a sense it stands as a visible reminder of the village's transition from agriculture to industry. Here, in 1770, lived John Field – a clothier. He can be regarded as the founding father of a dynasty which, until very recent times, played a major role in Skelmanthorpe's industrial life. The nearby sprawling Tentercroft Mills building was to be a significant part of that

Gill Gate, in Skelmanthorpe, dates from 1642. Here, in 1770, lived John Field – a clothier – who was to be the founding father of a dynasty which was, through its various branches, to play a very central role in the development of the village.

development. A few metres from 'Gill Gate' is the old Manor House, a late seventeenth century dwelling built originally for occupation by the steward of an absentee lord of the manor.

Like Clayton West, Skelmanthorpe is one of the villages which grew too rapidly for the parochial system of the Church of England to adapt, and so the nonconformist chapels are older than its parish church. The first active nonconformists were the Wesleyan Methodists who opened their chapel in 1816 and later replaced it with a larger, more substantial, building in 1895. Very little remains of that. Following an amalgamation between that church and the former Primitive Methodists in 1978, parts of the building have been demolished and the remainder has been converted into residential accomodation.

The Methodist Church in Pilling Lane was opened in 1836, but has subsequently undergone various acts of expansion and modernisation - especially in recent years when it has become the home of all Methodists in the village. Built originally for the Primitive Methodists, it housed a society that had been active in the village from the 1820s but which had been inhibited from fully establishing itself by

In 1800, the large house in the background was purchased by Joseph Field, son of John Field. Here Field and his three sons expanded Skelmanthorpe's textile industry. Weaving, dyeing and finishing all took place on one site. The Green is now commonly called 'The Triangle'.

considerable persecution.

The elegant Wesleyan Reform chapel of 1924, in Gib Lane, replaced an earlier building. The Wesleyan Reformers founded their society here in the 1850s and seem to have gained some impetus by an influx of disgruntled Wesleyan Methodists in the district. The source of their concern was in fact one of their own ministers, who appears to have been rather too 'fond of the bottle'. In one of his moments of inebriation he broke the windows of their chapel in Denby Dale.

Within what had become a nonconformist stronghold, the foundation stone of the Anglican parish church of St Aidan was laid by William Walsham How (the first Bishop of Wakefield) in 1894, and the gothic-style building was brought into use in the following year. Perhaps the most interesting historical feature within the building is the font. Standing on a modern stone base, its fairly primitive decorative carvings suggest that it is to be dated from at least the thirteenth century. It has had a chequered life. Having once stood in the church at High Hoyland, it was found at Wheatley Hill Farm, near Scissett, serving as a cattle feeding trough. After a period at Cannon Hall, Cawthorne, it was given to St Aidan's Church by the Spencer-Stanhope family of Cannon Hall, who had taken an active interest in the building of the church.

Two primary (or First) schools cater for village children – the Church of England school, near to St Aidan's, founded in 1864:

> for the education of children and adults of the labouring and manufacturing and other poor classes of the parish.

and, at the other end of the village (near to the Methodist Church) the former Board School which drew most of its early support from the nonconformists. Catering for many of the valley's older children is Shelley High School, opened as a comprehensive establishment in 1973.

Even the most cursory examination of the village will show that it has

Here and on the left: three early twentieth century views of Commercial Road – the main road passing through Skelmanthorpe.

The font in St Aidan's Church. Possibly of thirteenth century origin, it appears to have had a chequered career, having once stood in High Hoyland Church and later serving as a cattle feeding trough at Wheatley Hill Farm. It was given to St Aidan's Church by the Spencer-Stanhope family of Cannon Hall, Cawthorne.

developed many of the trappings of a small town. Shops, including a Co-op supermarket – the successor of one of the earliest co-operative societies founded in the Huddersfield district, in 1828 – banks, fire station, a former cinema, and other facilities in the central area, are now surrounded not only by the quaint stone cottages of two hundred years ago, but also by the larger estates of commuter dwellings. Also, along the Huddersfield Road, may be found the former offices of the Denby Dale Urban District Council for, until 1974, Skelmanthorpe was the centre of this unit of local government, serving a large part of the valley.

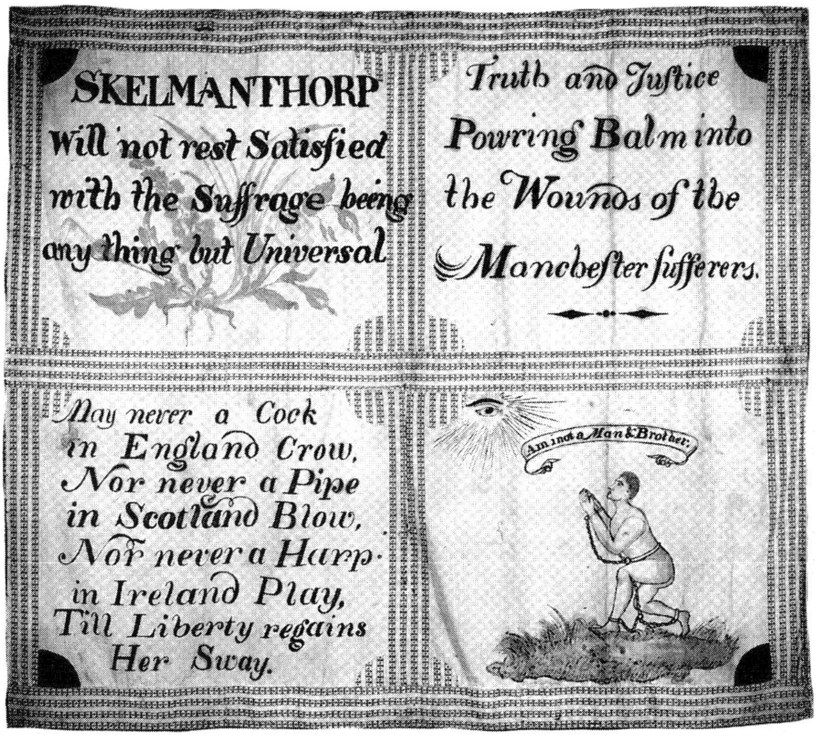

The Skelmanthorpe Flag.
Following the Peterloo Massacre in 1819, radical calls for the reform of Parliament were supported in the Huddersfield district. The flag was taken to many rallies, including those supporting the cause of Chartism. It is now preserved in the Tolson Museum in Huddersfield.

The Wind-Mill Inn in Skelmanthorpe in the early twentieth century – a hostelry which still provides a service to residents.

Former weavers' cottages in Lower Cumberworth.

Cumberworth

ON 16TH AUGUST 1773, Sir Thomas Blackett of Bretton Hall wrote to his brother-in-law, Godfrey Bosvile of Gunthwaite:

> I was upon Cumberworth and only got four birds; it was very hot and no wind ...

Standing on the heights of this settlement today, it is not easy to visualise the landscape with its dark stone-enclosed fields, farm buildings, terraced cottages and modern housing – interrupted by roads and lanes – as being the setting for an eighteenth century grouse shoot organised by the landed family of Bretton Hall; and, on the more exposed parts of the terrain, it can be rather difficult to imagine many days when it could have been very hot and without wind.

Divided into two communities – 'Upper' and 'Lower' – the predominantly rural area of Cumberworth seems to have been divided in its ownership for centuries, though the West Bretton family played a significant part in its affairs. Once renowned for the fine quality of its woven cloth, the village was largely left behind by the Industrial Revolution. Whilst power-looms and mills were being established in the valley bottom, so the weavers' cottages and the small-scale craftsmanship declined. So much was this the case that, in 1830, the parish curate (the Revd Charles Dunn) felt compelled to write to Diana Beaumont of Bretton Hall pleading for assistance for those suffering the effects of unemployment and poverty. Dunn was an interesting and noteworthy character. As curate of Cumberworth he ran the parish on behalf of the Rector, who lived in Penrith and never came to the village. He was a man of radical principle. Unusually for an Anglican clergyman of that period, he gave great support to the Co-operative movement and even looked forward to a time when capitalism would be replaced by, as he saw it, a fairer and more Christian ordering of society.

The Parish Church of St Nicholas, standing in Upper Cumberworth, is not the building that Dunn knew. A medieval building, which can be traced in documentary sources to the thirteenth century, was replaced in 1876. Within that older building, during the Commonwealth period of the seventeenth century, ministered perhaps one of the most notable clergymen in the whole of the valley – Henry Tilson, bishop of the Irish diocese of Elphin. Following a revolt of the Irish against the English, Tilson was driven from his diocese in 1645 and came to reside at Soothill Hall near Dewsbury. For several years, keeping a low profile in an age when bishops had been abolished, he travelled the twelve miles to Cumberworth each week to conduct services. Writing to a friend in 1651 he said:

> You shall know that I am not altogether idle, for I pray (after the Directory of the Church of England) and preach every Sunday at a place in the mountains called Cumberworth, two miles beyond Emley (where I have by the way Lawrence, my Hoste)..

Lawrence was Lawrence Farrington, Rector of Emley, who was a staunch Royalist. Tilson went on to say that the position had been offered to him by Thomas Wentworth of Bretton Hall, another staunch Royalist and patron of the Living of Cumberworth, and continued:

> because it came (as all my ecclesiastical livings and preferments have done) without my seeking and suit ..... I took it to be pointed out for me by God ..... though it will not reach to forty marks per annum .....

The Royalist Tilson continued by making some rather unflattering comments about the people of the district, who had shown Parliamentary sympathies:

> I trust to do God's service in the exercise of my ministry amongst that moorish and late rebellious people .....

One wonders how frequently some of the 'moorish' people may have suffered the indignity of being fastened in the stocks which still stand in the graveyard.

In Lower Cumberworth stands the chapel, built at a cost of £210 in 1851 for a society of Primitive Methodists. Two years after what appears to have been a fairly precarious foundation, it became the scene of a dispute in which the title deeds were seized by an offended party and the building was officially recorded as having been 'lost to the Connexion'. Five years were to pass before the matter was settled and the deeds returned – and it could then be reported that the chapel was 'got back'.

The stocks in Cumberworth Churchyard

The Wesleyan Reformers built their chapel in Upper Cumberworth in 1879. This has recently been converted into a private residence.

Dominating the village is one of its present industries – the manufacture of drain pipes. In 1901 a small brick works, utilising the fireclay found in the vicinity, developed into the Cumberworth Brick and Tile Company – the products of which were to be used nationwide. More recently, after a period of stagnation, the industry has been revitalised as part of a larger group of companies. The remains of various clay workings and several small coal mines bear testimony to the existence of small, family-owned, industries and crafts which have now disappeared.

All the villages in the vicinity have their own particular historical delights. Intriguing features of Cumberworth are the names of some of its roads and physical features. The origin of some seem to have been lost in the mists of antiquity. Why, for example, is Heresy Well Bottom so called? Amongst others, Ponker Lane, leading to Skelmanthorpe, may have originally indicated a pond or marshy ground in the vicinity, and Lane Hackings is probably derived from an ancient word which referred to 'hacking' or cultivating the soil.

Part of the spectacular stone viaduct of 1880 which carries the railway from Huddersfield to Sheffield over the River Dearne at Denby Dale.

Denby Dale

WITHIN THE HIGHER REACHES OF THE VALLEY, Denby Dale is yet another village which owes it development to nineteenth century industrial expansion. Known until the early years of that century as Denby Dike, it remained fairly isolated and rural until the building of the Barnsley and Shepley Lane Head turnpike road in 1824/5, and the Wakefield to Denby Dale turnpike road in 1825/6. Twenty-five years later came the railway, and cottage industries were steadily replaced by factories and mills.

Once again, textiles were dominant. In 1850 Zechariah Hinchliffe began to develop Hartcliffe Mills at the western edge of the village, and built up a reputation for the manufacture of woollen and worsted yarns. That enterprise still exists and, keeping a careful watch on the much-expanded business, is the millowner's residence on the slopes above the former Wakefield to Denby Dale turnpike road. Not far away, Jonas Kenyon began to manufacture 'fancy' goods and later worsted cloths in 1854 (a business which has now gone) and, in 1868, Messrs Brownhill and Scratchard set up their textile manufactury in Inkerman Mills, later moving to the more satisfactory Springfield Mill. This firm specialised in alpaca linings and then cotton brocades. During the Second World War some parachute silks and military khaki were produced here. But that business is no more. With the demise of textiles the mill has become, like Nortonthorpe, the home to several small businesses. Throughout the village are the stone terraced houses which housed the workforce for each of these concerns.

Another important industry involved the production of earthenware drainpipes and sanitary pipes by Naylor Brothers, a company which has had a long history within the village but has now moved its operations to Cawthorne. The Naylor family's connection with this locality began in 1877, when their tender of just over £27,000 was accepted for the building of the spectacular stone viaduct which crosses the valley at this point. The building (which bears a close examination of its design and sheer craftsmanship) was completed in 1880 and, in the following year, the family moved from the Cleckheaton district to live in a large house overlooking the successfully-completed project. Fireclay discovered in the vicinity, together with water, coal, and the

The old wooden railway viaduct is dismantled at Denby Dale, 1884-1885.

newly-developed transport systems, provided them with the resources that were needed to develop a successful business.

The viaduct with its 21 arches is quite breathtaking, and forms part of a railway system which posed many challenges in its construction. The thirteen and a half miles of track between Huddersfield and Penistone were opened in 1850. Six tunnels and four viaducts had been required. At Denby Dale the original viaduct was a wooden structure. Plans for it to be built in stone were discarded in the interest of financial restraint. Many people were uneasy about this. Even whilst it was being built, in January 1847, it suffered some gale damage. The *Sheffield Iris* newspaper commented:

> This structure altogether has such a cobweb appearance and is so unsuitable for the place and purpose intended that the public generally are well satisfied with its fall. It is to be hoped that, with this practical proof of the unstability of a wood viaduct, the directors will adopt the original plan and build a stone one .....

That hope was not to be fulfilled for some years. The wooden viaduct was completed. From then on it was seen by many as a serious fire risk. Each day, one of the porters at Denby Dale station was required to walk over it and top up to half-full the fire buckets that stood at regular intervals along the side of the track. Vibration from passing trains soon emptied them again. It was a great relief to many when, in 1880, the new stone viaduct was completed and the wooden remains were removed.

One notable Denby Dale personality of the past was John Firth, who was born at Leak Hall, between Denby Dale and Lower Cumberworth, in 1597. Following the Civil War and the establishment of the Commonwealth, Firth served in Cromwell's army and was sent to guard prisoners in Nottingham Castle. One of the inmates there was George Fox, the founder of the Society of Friends (Quakers), then an illegal movement suspected of subversion. Fox made such an impression on Firth that he was converted to Quakerism. On returning to the Dearne Valley he began to hold Quaker meetings. Two traditions have survived relating to his subsequent life. One states that soldiers were sent to apprehend him for his illegal activities, took him prisoner, and escorted him 'en route' to Halifax. He managed to escape from them, and hid in a nearby wood. The officer in charge of the escort was so angry that he shot his musket at a window of Kirkburton Vicarage, where he thought Firth was hiding. Unfortunately he shot Mrs Hester Whitaker, the wife of the Vicar. The other tradition (perhaps the more reliable) states that a cohort of Parliamentary soldiers came to Kirkburton during the night to arrest the vicar, the Revd Gamaliel Whitaker, who was a strong supporter of the monarchy and connected by marriage to several of the leading Royalist families in the North of England. Being uncertain of their way, the soldiers called on John Firth (then living at Shepley Hall just outside the valley) and ordered him to guide them to the vicarage. He was unwilling to do this and, whilst on the way to Kirkburton, managed to make his escape, hide in a nearby wood, and eventually return home. The soldiers arrived at the vicarage, and ordered Galmaliel Whitaker to appear at the door. His wife came downstairs to open the door and was shot by a trigger-happy soldier. (Whether that was intentional or an accident will probably never be known.) Whichever tradition is the more accurate, a number of facts are clear: Hester Whitaker was shot on 12th January 1644 and was buried in the churchyard at Kirkburton three days later; and John Firth was one of the leaders of Quaker activity in the district – leading and sustaining societies which prudently met in some secrecy in isolated places. (See the section on High Flatts).

As in the other industrial settlements in the valley, nonconformity became the first clearly-established form of Christianity in Denby Dale. The first such group were the Wesleyan Methodists who met in the textile mill and dyehouse of John Wood – the founding father of the society. Their first purpose-built chapel was opened in 1799 and

Denby Dale Methodist Church – built for a society of Wesleyan Methodists in 1799, and renovated and adapted several times since.

renovated and extended in 1877, again in 1899 and, more recently, in the 1970s. The former Primitive Methodist building on Miller Hill came into use in 1837 and was closed in 1962 when its members joined forces with the former Wesleyan Methodists. The Wesleyan Reformers opened their Zion chapel in 1860 and replaced it with a new building in Barnsley Road in 1908. In 1884 a corps of the Salvation Army – the only such group within the valley – was founded in a wooden hut in the village centre, and a more substantial building was opened in 1926. That building remains as a private residence, but the corps was disbanded in 1970. The situation had changed greatly from 25th July 1907 when General William Booth, the founder of the Salvation Army, made a visit to the village. Booth was by then 78 years of age, respected and warmly greeted on his travels throughout the country. In Denby Dale he was welcomed by local industrialists and leaders of community life, at a large gathering outside the then Prospect Hotel.

Denby Dale has never been a separate ecclesiastical parish, but was and remains part of the Parish of Cumberworth. It therefore does not have a parish church; but the Church of England is represented by Holy Trinity Church built in 1939. That replaced an iron building which had housed a congregation from 1893.

Amongst other public buildings in this substantial village is the former undenominational school (complete with master's house) and the Pie Hall, opened as a village hall on 5th September 1972.

Holy Trinity Church in Denby Dale

The Pie Hall is a visible reminder of a unique piece of tradition in village life. On ten occasions during the past 220 years, a huge pie has been baked as the centrepiece of much celebration. What was probably the first pie was baked in 1788 to mark the recovery of King George III from what had been perceived as mental illness. Thereafter, at infrequent intervals, further pies have been baked for a variety of reasons – to commemorate the victory at the Battle of Waterloo (1815); the Repeal of the Corn Laws (1846); Queen Victoria's Jubilee (1887); the fiftieth anniversary of the Repeal of the Corn Laws (1896); a belated First World War victory – in reality to raise money for Huddersfield Royal Infirmary (1928); the birth of four royal babies (1964); the bicentenary of the pie-baking tradition (1988); and the Millenium of 2000 – coupled with a commemoration of the centenary of Her Majesty Queen Elizabeth the Queen Mother. One is led to believe that almost any excuse has been sufficient to keep the tradition alive.

The 1964 pie was planned to be 'the world's largest pie.' It weighed some 6 tons which, when cut up and sold to the many visitors to the village, raised sufficient money to build the Pie Hall. The 1988 pie was again planned to be the largest ever. Its dish was made of mild steel and was twenty feet long. The dish alone weighed around half a ton and was designed to hold seven cubic metres of pie. The contents included 3000 kgs of English beef, 3000 kgs of potatoes, 700 kgs of onions, 700 kgs of gravy and spices, 1500 kgs of flour, and 1200 kgs of margarine.

It was in fact to be recorded in the Guinness Book of Records as the biggest meat and potato pie in the world. But even that was to be overshadowed by the Millenium Pie of 2000 – all 12.52 tonnes of it, containing the equivalent of 12 cows! A crowd of some 25,000 watched the 40 foot monster as it was paraded through the village, and then queued for three quarters of an hour to taste it.

Occasionally, and perhaps not surprisingly in such a large enterprise,

Denby Dale – centre of pie making on a gigantic scale.

disasters or near-disasters have occured. In 1928 the pie became stuck in the oven and it took over an hour for several men armed with ten-foot-length tram rails to lever it out and place it on the wagon that was to take it in procession through the village. Many years earlier, in 1846, when the pie was placed on a temporary platform where various dignitaries were assembled, the weight became too much and the platform collapsed. The pie was virtually destroyed, though people surged forward and grabbed pieces of it. But the biggest disaster came in 1887 when the Golden Jubilee Pie was cut open and found to be inedible. The crowds who had flocked to the site in eager anticipation quickly dispersed and, on Sunday August 28th, the remains were buried in quicklime. The sad occasion was marked by the issue of funeral cards and appropriate verses:

> Tho' lost to sight, yet still to memory dear
> We smell it yet as tho' it still was here;
> Tho' short its life and quick was its decay,
> We thought it best to bury it without the least delay.
>
> Strong, strong was the smell that compelled us to part
> From a treat to our stomach and a salve to our heart;
> Like the last Denby Pie which the crowd did assail,
> Its contents a rank mixture, it quickly turned stale.
> Though we could not eat, yet we still lingered near,
> Till the stench proved too much for our nasals to bear;
> So like sensible men the committee did say:
> "Twas better to inter it without further delay."

Undeterred, the villagers set to work, in September of that same year, to produce a second version which became known as the 'Resurrection Pie'.

When Wakefield lawyer W.S. Banks wrote about his walks in the Denby Dale district in 1871, he expressed his interest both in the pie-making tradition and the distinctive dialect of the district (which still exists):

> Take as a specimen of the Denby Dale talk, the following, which was spoken by a native as we passed through the village one day and were looking about. Looking he thought, at a particular field: 'That's t'field wheere t'big pawoi (pie) wor. Theere wor three whaul sheep an a cawf (calf) e wun pawoi. What wor it for? Whawoi, rejoicin at Corn Bill cummin off e 46. T'pawoi weighed ten hundred weight. They lawoik (like) pawoi, mun, e Denby Dale .....'

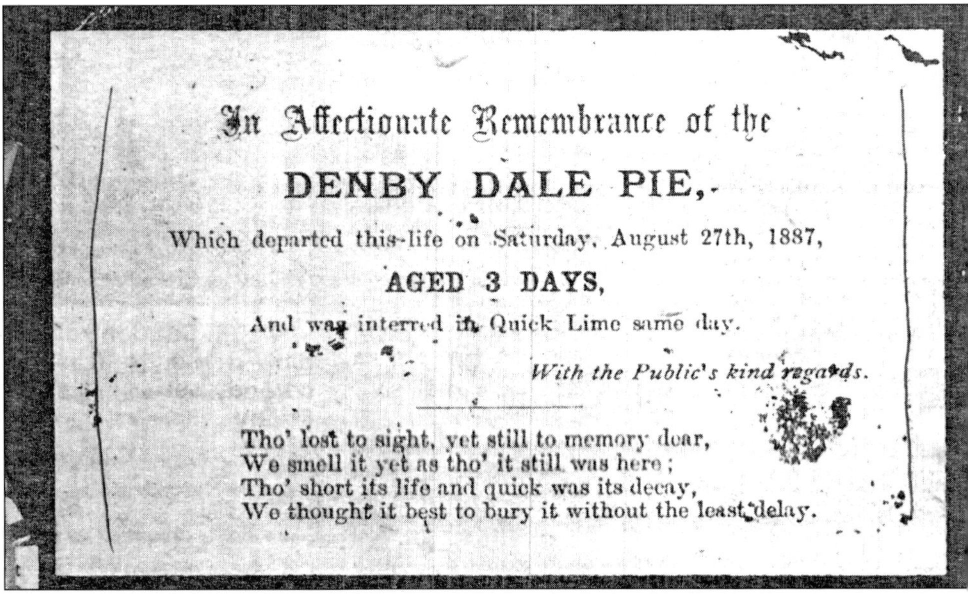

In Affectionate Remembrance of the

DENBY DALE PIE,

Which departed this-life on Saturday, August 27th, 1887,

AGED 3 DAYS,

And was interred in Quick Lime same day.

With the Public's kind regards.

Tho' lost to sight, yet still to memory dear,
We smell it yet as tho' it still was here;
Tho' short its life and quick was its decay,
We thought it best to bury it without the least delay.

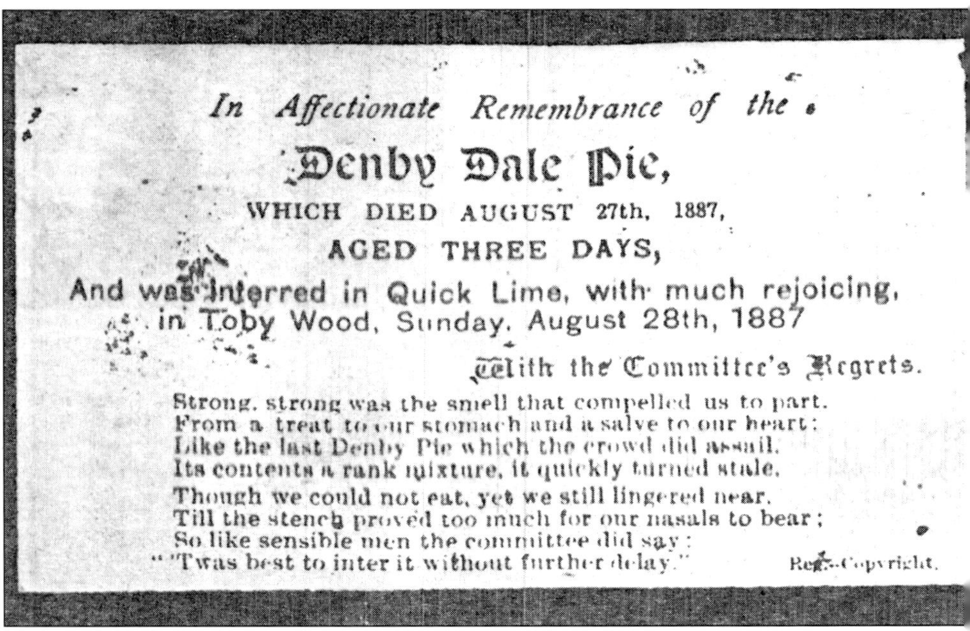

In Affectionate Remembrance of the

Denby Dale Pie,

WHICH DIED AUGUST 27th, 1887,

AGED THREE DAYS,

And was interred in Quick Lime, with much rejoicing,
in Toby Wood, Sunday, August 28th, 1887

With the Committee's Regrets.

Strong, strong was the smell that compelled us to part,
From a treat to our stomach and a salve to our heart;
Like the last Denby Pie which the crowd did assail,
Its contents a rank mixture, it quickly turned stale.
Though we could not eat, yet we still lingered near,
Till the stench proved too much for our nasals to bear;
So like sensible men the committee did say:
"'Twas best to inter it without further delay."

Regd.-Copyright.

PROGRAMMES ONE PENNY EACH.

Denby Dale Jubilee Pie, 1896.

This Pie is in Commemoration of the Repeal of the Corn Laws, 1846.

The oven is designed, and constructed by Messrs. Allott Bros., of Denby Dale, and its dimensions are 13ft. long 9 feet wide and 2ft. high (inside measurement), and is situated adjacent to Mr. F. Horn's, Corn Mill, by his kind permission.

The dish, which is made of ⅜ inch. steel plates, is 10ft. long, 6ft. 5in. wide and 1ft. deep, has been specially made by Messrs. W. C. Holmes & Co., Huddersfield, and weighs about ½ ton.

The contents of the Pie are as follows:—

Beef 1120 lbs., Veal 180 lbs., Mutton 112 lbs., Lamb 60 lbs., Flour 1120 lbs., and Lard 160 lbs.

The gross weight of dish and contents is about 35 cwts.

The Pie has been prepared by a few ladies in the village, assisted by Messrs. J. W. Spivey, and F. Dearnley, Denby Dale.

The Carvers which are of a very elegant design, with buck horn handles, and silver-mountings, have been supplied by Mr. Wm. Lockwood, Jeweller, &c., Victoria Lane, Huddersfield. The knife is 33 inches long (with suitable inscription on blade), and the fork 25 inches long.

The Proceeds realized from the Celebration, after all expenses have been paid, will be devoted to Local Charities.

ENJOY YOUR SLICE OF THE ACTION

WITHOUT A SHARE OF THE TRAFFIC

The specially made dish for the Denby Dale pie of 1964 now serves as a container for flowers near to the entrance to the Pie Hall.

Transport for the largest pie in the world, at Denby Dale, in 1928.

The namepate of the farmstead on the outskirts of Denby Dale acts as a reminder of what was once a flourishing textile trade in the district. Over many years, as part of the production process, woollen cloth was dried and stretched in the open air on tenter frames. By the early nineteenth century, tenter houses were built to provide indoor drying, using warm air from steam or gas.

High Flatts and Birdsedge

AT THE VERY HEAD OF THE VALLEY stand these two small hamlets which seem to run into each other. The word 'Flatt' is medieval in origin, and refers to groups of selions (strips) in cultivated ground. If that be the case, then those who cultivated the ground here, so long ago, were both brave and optimistic for, at 300 metres above sea-level, the Flatts are high and exposed to all weathers. Today it is difficult to picture anything other than grassland and grazing, but the fact that it is exposed and bleak is probably part of the reason why what appears to have been a fortified settlement was constructed some 4,000 or more years ago. Little can now be seen on the surface after centuries of cultivation – apart from the hill known locally as 'Castle Hill' and marked on Ordnance Survey maps as 'Earthwork'. The site awaits a full excavation, but numerous fragments of ancient flint waste, and sorne tools, have been found there – some of which may be seen in the Tolson Memorial Museum in Huddersfield. Who lived here, and how did they occupy themselves? For the moment we can do little other than imagine and speculate. What does seem clear is that the site was abandoned in the early years of the first century of the Christian era – possibly as Roman soldiers marched northwards, establishing England as an outpost of their empire.

About half a mile away, at the eastern side of the Huddersfield to Penistone road, down a short lane, is 'Quaker Bottom', a small settlement which has been the local meeting place for members of the Religious Society of Friends (Quakers) since the end of the seventeenth century. The Quakers were organised as a distinctive religious group by George Fox in 1668. In their early days they suffered constant persecution; and indeed, more recently, their refusal to take part in military service or swear oaths has brought them into conflict with civil authorities. Amongst local members of the society so harrassed was Richard Priest of Denby (who was imprisoned for attending a Quaker meeting in 1660) and Joshua Green, also of Denby (who was committed to York Castle in 1682 for refusing to take the Oath of Allegiance). On the other hand, their devotion to social and educational work, and their high standards of integrity and morality, gradually brought respect and admiration. 'Quaker Bottom' provides a visible illustration of both these facets of their life. It was built in what would originally have been a very secluded spot which, it may be assumed, gave a certain degree of security, and within the complex of buildings were once a boarding school and a sanatorium for inebriate women.

Part of the complex of buildings which form '**Quaker Bottom**' at High Flatts.

Numerous visitors to this place have commented on its peacefulness. It is almost as if time has stood still. As one wanders around the cobbled streets, now a residential hamlet for those who delight in rural life and from which superb views of the Dearne Valley may be seen, the dominant building is the meeting house itself. A barn given by a sympathetic farmer in 1701 became the base, and this was rebuilt in 1750. The interior is very simple: wooden benches, a central table and a Bible – as befits a form of religious practice which involves no ceremony, no clergy and no pre-arranged services. Outside is a typical Quaker burial ground, with its uniform unpretentious stones symbolically proclaiming belief in the equality of all people before

God. 'Quaker Bottom' served as a religious centre for a very large area, with a congregation of about one hundred in the late nineteenth century. It still serves a large area, but with a much reduced attendance. That part of the A629 road running through High Flatts and Birdsedge was originally built by John Metcalfe (popularly known as 'Blind Jack of Knaresborough'). He was an amazing man. Having lost his sight through an attack of smallpox when he was six years old, he went on to become one of the great road builders of thc Industrial Revolution. In his lifetime he oversaw the construction of some 200 miles of roads, often in the most hazardous of situations, in many parts of Northern England. His usual procedure was to survey possible routes and use a long stick to ascertain what the ground surface was like. He would then put down layers of heather to provide a foundation for locally-quarried

The Quaker Meeting House which lies at the centre of the community.

The interior of the Friends' Meeting House at High Flatts.

The simple burial ground outside the Meeting House.

stone and rubble. Every aspect of the work was supervised by him – even the supply of provisions to his workforce.

Birdsedge is a small village situated very near to the river's source at Dearne Head, and dominated by the textile mill to which it owes its existence. As a village it does not appear to have a very long history. Most of its houses were, in fact, built to accommodate the mill's workforce, and are interspersed with one or two older farmsteads.

The original mill was established by the Dickensons – a prominent Quaker family living here in the eighteenth and nineteenth centuries. According to the Visitation Returns of Archbishop Herring of York, compiled in 1743, Elihu Dickenson was a 'teacher' in the Quaker meeting-house at High Flatts. Subsequent generations of the family appear in various records as active Quakers, landowners, clothing manufacturers, and as supporters of charitable works on behalf of the poor. More than once has the mill gone through precarious times and, since 1921, it has been a component in the company of Z. Hinchliffe of Denby Dale.

The village hall was once a school established by the Quaker families of the district. It was replaced in 1911 by the present local authority primary school – a building which has been renovated and extended at various times since. Outside the school a pleasant garden and sun-dial are reminders of the coronation of Her Majesty Queen Elizabeth II in 1953.

Ecclesiastically, the village has been divided by the river between the parishes of Denby and Cumberworth, and it was to those parish churches that Anglican villagers traditionally turned for baptisms, marriages and funerals. The Wesleyan Reformers, however, managed to establish a presence here – the only nonconformist body to do so. After meeting in each other's homes, they were able to build a chapel in 1868 - a building which is still in use.

Denby

DIVIDED INTO UPPER AND LOWER DENBY, it has already been noted that, in the Domesday Book of 1086, it is the only Yorkshire village stated to have possessed a cattle farm ('vaccary'). That is not to say, of course, that no others existed in such a large county. One can probably assume that they did but, for whatever reason, remained unrecorded. The village has remained very much an agricultural settlement ever since.

By the late eighteenth century a considerable number of weavers were established here – usually combining their industry with their agriculture in what was essentially a cottage-based occupation. As in Cumberworth, the many changes that were to come about in the nineteenth century expansion and reorganisation of the textile industry brought hardship and unemployment to a number of families. In 1826, for instance, at a meeting chaired by the Quaker Elihu Dickenson, 127 families were reported to be suffering the effects of poverty. It was decided that a subscription should be raised to assist them. In 1827, rather more ignominiously, a workhouse for the village's paupers was established – a building which no longer exists. The industry, nevertheless, survived – at least in the short term. According to the 1851 Census, some 118 villagers were textile manufacturers or weavers. The demise came in the second half of the nineteenth century with the building of mills in Denby Dale and elsewhere. The cottagers' weaving looms became redundant, and working people now had to travel away from the village to earn their livelihood.

Historically Denby lay within the ecclesiastical parish of Penistone and, in order to reach their parish church, parishioners had to make a long and arduous journey. In 1626, following a tragedy in which thirteen parishioners were drowned in the flood-waters of Scout Dike whilst on their way to Penistone, a petition was presented to the Archbishop of York seeking permission to build a chapel-of-ease in the village. Permission was granted and, in the following year, a building was erected. Godfrey Bosvile of nearby Gunthwaite Hall was instrumental in bringing this about. The chapel was the forerunner of the present parish church of St John, though only the tower of that earlier building remains. The upper part of the tower was rebuilt in 1957.

The Parish Church of St John, Denby

The Bosviles were Puritans – that austere form of extreme Protestantism which sought purification of the church from supposedly unscriptural and corrupt practices. They ensured that a succession of Puritan clergy exercised pastoral leadership in the village, beginning with the Revd Charles Broxholme – 'a very zealous Puritan minister'. The village was visited more than once by the Revd Oliver Heywood, the great exponent of Puritanism in the West Riding of Yorkshire. Hospitality was provided for him by members of the Cotton family, ironmasters in the district whose house was, for a time, licensed as a Puritan meeting place.

In 1839 Denby was visited by its diocesan bishop, then Charles Longley, Bishop of Ripon – later to become Archbishop of Canterbury. On a similar pastoral visit, to Haworth, he had stayed with the Brontes at the parsonage, before it had developed into the literary shrine it was to become. Writing about the bishop, Charlotte Bronte said:

> He is certainly a most charming bishop, the most benignant gentleman that ever put on lawn sleeves, yet stately too and competent to check encroachments ...

Whatever she meant by the latter phrase, he certainly seems to have been direct and efficient. What he found in Denby disturbed him. He seems to have considered the chapel-of-ease to be dilapidated, dirty and ruinous – the worst in the diocese! He ordered that it should be demolished and money raised to rebuild it. Amazingly, that happened. In 1845 John Ellis, a builder from High Flatts, was able to complete a new church at a cost of £1,170. The nave of that building survives, a chancel and vestry being added to it in 1901.

Denby became an independent parish in 1853, embracing not only the immediate village but also the communities of Gunthwaite, Ingbirchworth, High Flatts, part of Birdsedge and part of Denby Dale. At the present time, following a reorganisation of parish boundaries, it is part of a united parish of Cumberworth and Denby.

The Wesleyan Reformers appear to have been the only Methodist group to establish themselves in the village, and they turned out to be rather ephemeral. They built a chapel in 1911, but it was closed in 1930 and survives, in the centre of the village, as a private residence.

The village school was built in 1864 and allied to the National Society. It was not the first educational enterprise here, however. Apart from the Quaker school in Birdsedge which would have drawn some pupils from Denby, a charity school had existed in Lower Denby since the eighteenth century. Endowed by Francis Burdett of Denby Hall (a building which is now a farmhouse), it survived until the 1860s. Like the Wesleyan Reform chapel, the building is now a dwelling house.

In 1674 Denby was the centre of a certain amount of notoriety, when allegations of the practice of witchcraft became public knowledge. Two local women who were mother and daughter, Ann Shillitoe and Susan Hinchliffe, were charged and taken to the court in Barnsley. Their accuser was Mary Moor, a sixteen-year-old girl from Clayton West. She claimed that she had heard a conversation between the two women, in which Hinchliffe had suggested that it was possible to gain power over another person's life and property by performing certain ritual acts, such as touching hair or staring hard into the face. She had claimed that she herself had brought about misfortune to several people, including the destruction of two pigs and hurt to a child. The situation became rather more complex when, during the trial, Mary Moor was herself accused of evil practices. It was said that she had vomited 'a piece of bended wire and a piece of paper with two crooked pins in it ..... and hath at several other times been seen to vomit crooked pins.' It has been suggested that what lay behind this gruesome little story was a long-standing feud between two families in which gossip and innuendo were a central part of trying to 'score points' over enemies. In sixteenth and seventeenth century England, charges of witchcraft were fairly commonplace. Under an Act of James I, witches were to be condemned to death without the benefit of clergy. The truth was often distorted to suit those who were making the allegations, and a great deal of hysteria was aroused. In the event, it appears that a petition was presented to the magistrates, signed by some fifty people, pleading the innocence of Shillitoe and Hinchliffe, and castigating Mary Moor. Following usual practice, the two women were committed to the Assizes at York. The evidence is not then entirely clear. Either the case was thrown out before trial or, more probably, the women were brought to trial and acquitted. Women charged with this kind of offence in Yorkshire were usually acquitted.

In the early years of the nineteenth century another Denby woman, Betty Roberts, was also referred to as a witch:

> She was very peculiar looking, and wore a tall peaked bonnet or hat, and a long dark cloak something after the familiar pictures of Mother Shipton. She lived in a lone hut, which the boys were terrified to pass, although there was a strange attraction to try and peep in, for they were taught they might see the "posnet" or small cauldron on the fire, in which she brewed the 'stuff' by which she was enabled to fly up the chimney or through the keyhole. When she was teased she made strong cabalistic signs, as if she were calling the stars to avenge her, at the same time uttering some strange gibberish. As she had no relatives, it was supposed that at one time she had belonged to a wandering tribe of gypsies.

Fortunately, perhaps, the residents of the village today have a more informed and rational approach to life. What once was a rather remote place, in which legends and traditions could flourish, has given way to a commuter settlement which provides a bracing and wholesome atmosphere for those whose work lies in the numerous urban centres of West and South Yorkshire.

Gunthwaite

A SHORT DISTANCE OUTSIDE THE VILLAGE OF DENBY, on one of the Dearne's tributaries, almost hidden in its tree-sheltered valley, lies Gunthwaite. This delightful spot may not now show many visible physical remains, but it has a long and complex historical story. In Saxon times the people here were simply known as 'de Gunnilthwaite', and so it remained until, some time in the fourteenth century, a family called Bosville took possession of their estate. Descendants of an officer who came over to England from Normandy in the army of William the Conqueror, they entered into ownership by making what seems to have been a prudent marriage with the last female descendant of the 'de Gunnilthwaite' line. They remained as owners, though not always residing here, until 1813. History then repeated itself, for when the last of the Bosville males died the estate passed to his sister who had married into the family of Macdonald of Sleet. The Macdonalds retained the property until 1952, when they sold out. Eleven years later, the estate was sold again and passed into the hands of another member of the Macdonald family. He retained it until 1982 when the trappings of the former feudal system were finally thrown away. The tenants were able to purchase their various properties and become their own masters.

Little remains of Gunthwaite Hall – a seventeenth century building. What does remain is now divided into two farmhouses. Apparently it was not the most comfortable house in which to live and, sometime during the eighteenth century, the Bosvilles moved to what they considered to be a more desirable residence at Thorpe, near to the East Riding town of Beverley. They did not, however, immediately relinquish their stewardship here, as has already been shown. One commentator has noted:

> the temptations of a modern house erected to their hands at Thorpe seduced them to move thither and Gunthwaite soon abandoned to tenants began to sink .....

How far it sank is difficult to assess, for most of the residence was demolished during the nineteenth century by the Bosvilles' agent –

Part of the former Gunthwaite Hall building

popularly known as 'Mad Earnshaw'.

Several outbuildings remain, showing signs of their former grandeur and bearing date stones and carved initials of members of the Bosville family. A two-storyed summer house, complete with chimney and weather vane, is located in what was once the front garden. At the rear are the remains of a large oak tree beneath which, tradition declares, are buried a large number of Oliver Cromwell's men who stopped off at Gunthwaite during the Civil War and died from sickness.

The most splendid feature at Gunthwaite is the barn – a superb example of sixteenth century craftsmanship and one of the finest such structures for many miles around. A long stone and timber building (now divided into two), it consists of eleven bays, with magnificent oak posts and beams held together by wooden pegs which are believed to have been carved by one of the apprentice builders who worked there. It is said that the task of making the pegs kept him at work for the

The noteworthy timbered barn at Gunthwaite. Now divided into two barns, it provides a superb example of sixteenth century craftsmanship

whole of his apprenticeship. There are six barn doors – three on each side of the building. Each one was reputely wide enough for 'a wain with six oxen to turn in it'.

A stone-flagged path leads from the site of the hall to Gunthwaite dam and spa. The Spa well, which has been renovated in recent years, became well known for the peculiar taste of its water and its supposed healing properties. The first Sunday in May is known as Spa Sunday and, at one time, it was a holiday for farm labourers in the district. Celebrations attracted many hundreds of people with feasting, singing and dancing. Today, the celebration is a rather smaller-scale event, but it still takes place – weather permitting.

Near to the dam is the water-powered corn mill where farmers from medieval times took their corn to be ground. It continued in use until as recently as 1956. The water-wheel survives – together with the drying kiln and grinding mechanism.

The remains of an ancient oak tree at Gunthwaite. According to popular tradition a large number of Oliver Cromwell's soldiers were buried on this site during the Civil War.

Cawthorne

STANDING IN WHAT HAS BEEN DESCRIBED AS a 'picture-postcard village', and observing neat, well-kept houses set against a background of parkland and agriculture, it is difficult to comprehend that Cawthorne was once an important industrial centre. By the end of the eighteenth century more people here earned their livelihood from coal mining, the production of iron, leather tanning, and numerous allied trades and crafts, than from agriculture. It is also difficult to understand that, just outside the village, at Barnby Basin, was the busy terminus of a branch of the Barnsley Canal, fed by wagonways laid down from the district's collieries. Coal was an important 'export' from here and, in 1820, over 10,000 tons were handled. The canal has long-since gone and the basin is now virtually non-existent, being almost sliced in two by the Ml motorway, and overgrown. Little remains of the industrial buildings that once clustered around it.

Whilst the lordship of the manor of Cawthorne passed through such families as the Nevilles, the Watertons, the Wentworths and the Beaumonts – all prominent gentry families in the county – and parts of the village were owned by members of the Bosville family, it was to the Spencer-Stanhopes that the village increasingly looked for support and leadership. The dynasty began when John Spencer, a maker of hay rakes, arrived in the district from Montgomeryshire round about 1660. An astute businessman, he was able to purchase the furnace and forge at Barnby; and so began the development of a remarkable business empire which, by the eighteenth century, had matured into a complex of furnaces, forges, mills, mines and woods (for charcoal) spreading out over some 800 square miles of the country. To add to his achievements, he married the heir to the Cannon Hall Estate. Fortune seemed to smile on him in every way!

Three generations of the Spencer family consolidated their holdings in the immediate district and elsewhere, but the last male heir – another John Spencer, died unmarried in 1775. His sister Ann had married Walter Stanhope of Horsforth, and it was to be their son, also called Walter, who inherited Cannon Hall – changing his surname in the process to Spencer-Stanhope. Successive generations of Spencer-Stanhopes continued to live at Cannon Hall until 1951, entering not

Cannon Hall at Cawthorne – the former home of the Spencer-Stanhope family

only into local life but occasionally into county and national affairs. The last male heir died in 1944 and it was his daughter, Mrs Fraser Spencer-Stanhope, who sold the house to Barnsley Corporation. It was subsequently converted into the museum and country park found there today.

The Revd Joseph Hunter, the great Yorkshire antiquarian of the nineteenth century, suggested that the name Cannon Hall was probably derived from the name of Gilbert Canun of Birthwaite in the the early part of the fourteenth century – that name occuring, he pointed out, in some of the earliest Cawthorne deeds. What may have originally been a small fortified house was rebuilt in stages during the eighteenth and nineteenth centuries. The central part of the main house had been constructed by 1720. East and west wings of one storey each were added in 1765, designed by John Carr the celebrated Yorkshire architect. Additional storeys were added to the wings in 1804/5, and in 1890/1 a splendid ballroom was added on the north side of the house.

About 1761 John Spencer began the process of landscaping the park, employing Richard Woods – a nurseryman and landscape architect from Surrey. This involved the construction of three lakes, a palladian bridge, and the planting of some 217 varieties of trees.

There has been a church in Cawthorne since Saxon times. Several fragments of stone crosses of that era may be found in the outer walls of the chancel of the present building, and in a reconstructed cross in the graveyard. The church as it is now seen is, in essence, a thirteenth century building – much modified and repaired at various times since. The Lady Chapel was probably the Chantry of Our Lady which was founded by Isabel Bosville in 1454. Between 1875 and 1880 two of the Spencer-Stanhopes, Walter and Roddam, financed a major restoration

All Saints' Church at Cawthorne. The reconstructed cross in the foreground contains a number of fragments of Saxon crosses.

as a memorial to their parents. Roddam was a talented artist associated with the Pre-Raphaelites, and he was particularly responsible for the design of the west window and the decorated panels on the pulpit. Other examples of his work are to be found on the pulpit in Denby Parish Church and, further afield, in the Oxford Union building and in the chapel of Marlborough College. Cawthorne Church remained as a chapelry within the parish of Silkstone until 1608, when it became the centre of a newly created parish.

The nearby Parish Room was once Cawthorne Grammar School. Like several other similar schools in the former West Riding of Yorkshire, its history can be traced back to medieval times when it was established in connection with the Chantry of Our Lady in the church. It has been noted earlier that chantries were a strong feature of medieval religious life, endowed primarily so that priests could regularly offer prayers for the souls of their departed founders. Not surprisingly, they had become increasingly popular after the death and devastation caused by the Black Death. Wealth and piety, combined with more than a dash of superstition, was poured into them. Since the chantry priest usually had no parochial responsibility, he sometimes taught pupils – partly to supplement his income and partly to occupy his time. When chantries were dissolved at the time of the Reformation, the school was reconstituted as a Grammar School for boys. For some years the boys continued to be taught in the church – until a purpose-built school was

The Parish Room at Cawthorne – formerly the village's Grammar School

Barnby Hall was built in 1820 on the site of an older residence which had been destroyed by fire. Here had lived the Barnby family, whose considerable estate was sold to the Spencers in the early eighteenth century.

brought into use in 1639. The older parts of the Parish Room were that school. The Grammar School maintained its existence until 1862 – though gradually declining in status. In that year it became associated with the National Society. In 1872 the present village school was built for the education of boys, and the Grammar School building became an infants' school. Education for girls had been provided by the Spencer-Stanhopes from 1858 in the building in Tivydale which is now the village hall. It was not to be until the 1930s that all the village's schoolchildren were brought together in the one school.

To the east of the village stands Barnby Hall, the present house being built in the early years of the nineteenth century. The site was originally the home of the Barnby family who were once very influential in Cawthorne and beyond. During the Civil War they suffered as a consequence of supporting the Royalist cause, and it was to be their estate that was sold to the Spencer family in the early eighteenth century.

Bamby Furnace was situated to the south of the former Barnsley-Shepley Lane Head turnpike road (the present A635). In the seventeenth century local resources – ironstone, wood for charcoal and water for power – had provided all that was needed for the development of a flourishing concern, but 100 years later the situation had changed. The ironstone was becoming exhausted and charcoal-

Cawthorne Methodist Church (formerly Wesleyan Methodist) opened in 1896

fuelled furnaces were becoming increasingly out of fashion. Following the Darby developments in Shropshire, coke was to be the fuel of the future. An attempt was made to convert Barnby Furnace at a cost of some £744. This was an expensive operation, but one that must have been thought to be viable at a time when there was a demand for munitions. The American War of Independence and the later unrest caused by the French Revolution led to the manufacture of cannon balls in Cawthorne. This was to be the last gasp of a dying enterprise. By 1815 the local iron industry was gone, and the numerous partnerships into which the Spencers had entered were dissolved.

As in the other industrial villages in the valley, nonconformity was able to stimulate a following, to a degree, in Cawthorne. The Puritan preacher Oliver Heywood visited the village several times in the 1670s, and was provided with hospitality by local people. Before the end of the eighteenth century, Methodist preachers had received support and established a society and, in subsequent years, several of the various sub-divisions of that movement – Methodist New Connexion, Primitive Methodists and Wesleyan Reformers – had gained a foothold – albeit not long-lasting. The present Methodist Church in Darton Road was opened in 1896, replacing a cottage meeting place. In contrast to some other Estate villages, the landowning family, the Spencer-Stanhopes, were not hostile to this development. A contemporary writer noted:

> All the land in the neighbourhood belongs to Colonel Spencer-Stanhope CB, who has shown unfailing kindness to all his tenants and not least to those who are of the people called Methodists .....

Not only were they not hostile; they actually made a donation to the building project in addition to giving the land.

Amongst many other interesting features in a village which has guarded so much of its heritage, two stand out. The Victoria Jubilee Museum was opened in 1887 with a great deal of support from Roddam Spencer-Stanhope and the then Vicar of Cawthorne, the Revd C.T. Pratt. In 1953 it was purchased from the Cannon Hall Estate and vested in a body of trustees. In many ways the museum is unique and houses not only objects brought back from their foreign travels by the Spencer-Stanhopes, but many items and curios of intense local interest. In what other museum could you find a stuffed two-headed lamb (from the farm at Gunthwaite Hall), a 9lb 6oz gall stone taken from a horse, or the

Cawthorne's Fountain Cross, erected in 1866 to commemorate the bringing of a piped water supply into the village.

remains of a pair of boots worn by a villager when he was struck by lightning? Not far away is the Fountain Cross in Church Street, which commemorates the bringing of a piped water supply into the village from a nearby wood. The stone cross, given by members of the Spencer-Stanhope family was erected in 1866. That this small feat of engineering meant a great deal to village people was shown by the fact that, in 1867, a public tea was held for some 300 of them to celebrate its completion. Not that it meant the luxury of a piped water supply being laid to each house; that was not to happen for another 40 years!

Cawthorne village once had three licensed drinking-places including The Golden Cross – now a private residence.

High Hoyland

REFERRED TO IN THE DOMESDAY BOOK as being in the possession of Ailric, lord of several estates in South Yorkshire both before and after the Conquest, this ancient village stands some 183 metres above sea-level, with outstanding views of West and South Yorkshire, and further afield to the Peak District. By the fourteenth century it had passed into the hands of the Burdet family, who also held the lordship of Denby

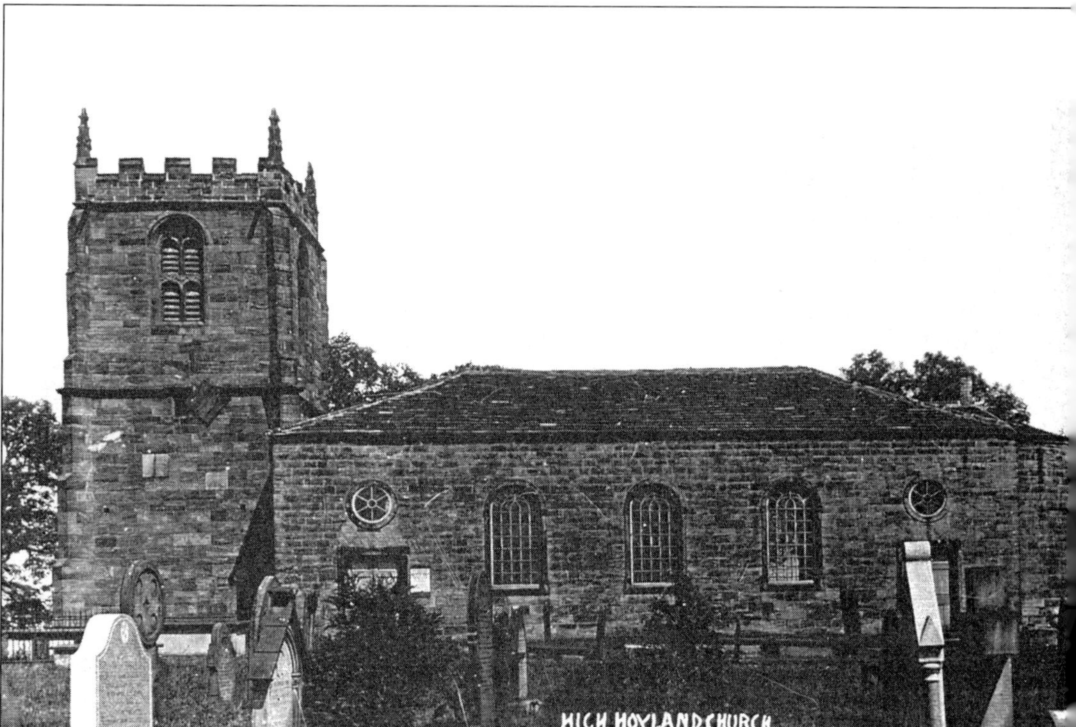

High Hoyland Church as it appeared from 1804 to 1904. The tower was built in 1679 and still remains as a prominent landmark in the district.

and were seated at Birthwaite Hall near Darton. As a consquence of severe financial difficulties brought about by profligate living, Francis Burdet sold High Hoyland to Sir Matthew Wentworth of Bretton Hall in the late seventeenth century. The village remained part of the Bretton Estate until 1958.

High Hoyland never seems to have been very large, though it was to be the centre of a very large parish embracing much of Bretton Park, the whole of Clayton West and Scissett, and parts of Skelmanthorpe and Cumberworth. During the eighteenth and nineteenth centuries, industrial developments in the valley, together with associated population movements, meant that the village was left very much on the edge of activity. Each nineteenth century census return recorded a decrease in population. In 1801 it had stood at 270; by 1951 it was down to almost half that figure. The village, therefore, missed some of the uglier developments that industry stimulated. What industry there was here remained very small-scale. Some coal-mining took place. In 1768 Sir Thomas Wentworth agreed to two men, John Waites and John Dyson, mining for one year at a rental of £9; in 1790 a lease was granted to Richard Stringer and William Dyson to work a colliery, but to employ only four men. In 1794 William Field (the village constable), Stephen Green (the licensee of the Cherry Tree Inn), and William Dyson (a local farmer) were similarly granted a lease; and in the 1860s Joseph Norton of Scissett was mining coal for his Nortonthorpe Mills. The scanty remains of some of these developments can still be seen.

It is quite possible (though not yet proved) that an Iron Age settlement was to be found here some 2000 years ago, and that a pre-Christian worship centre was established near to where the church now stands. What seems reasonably clear is that there was a preaching centre of some kind in the earliest stages of Christian expansion in the area – perhaps no more than a stone cross which marked the spot where the missionaries might address the people. When the first actual church building was erected is impossible to say, but in about 1150 Adam Fitz Swain – a prolific church builder, built a church here and dedicated it to All Hallows. Nothing substantial remains of that building. The oldest part of the present building is the perpendicular tower dating from 1679. Fitz Swain's church was demolished in 1804 and replaced with a larger building – Georgian in style but extremely plain and rather uninspiring. That was replaced in 1904-8 by the present building, when stones from the earlier churches were incorporated, including

High Hoyland Church undergoing rebuilding in 1907 (above), and the completed Church (below). Only the seventeenth century tower remained undisturbed.

fragments of Anglo-Saxon crosses inserted into the internal north wall. It has already been seen that High Hoyland Church ceased to be a parish church in 1875 when all the rights and privileges of a parish church were transferred to Clayton West. The building is no longer in use as a church, but is now administered by Bretton Hall University College.

In many respects the graveyard is perhaps the most interesting (and certainly the most historical) feature of the site. Not only does it appear to have been the site of a beacon in days when national states of emergency were made known by lighting bonfires, but its handsome tombstones provide a doorway into an understanding of the social composition of the population of the parish, as well as an insight into beliefs and practices. The patient explorer will discover the tombstone of Ann Copley – born in 1600 and living, according to the inscription, to the ripe old age of 105. She is also stated to have given birth to her last child at the age of fifty. On the tombstone of Joseph Dawson of Bretton West, who died in 1859, is the stark message:

> Look Here young Man as You Pass By
> A blooming Youth as once was I;
> As I am now, so You must be;
> Prepare in Time to Follow me.

and, not far away, the same sentiments are further expressed:

The former Primitive Methodist Chapel in High Hoyland – built in 1890. One hundred years later it was converted into a private residence.

High Hoyland Hall – built about 1720 to replace a Tudor dwelling.

Here lies he,
that was as ye
And ye as he shall shortly be.

The Primitive Methodists appear to have been the only nonconformist group to have been active in the village. They were able to build a chapel in 1890 beside the road that leads to Cawthorne. It is now a private residence.

The most distinguished secular building in the village is the magnificent Queen Anne style hall built about 1720, replacing a Tudor dwelling. According to popular tradition, that Tudor house had been haunted. A family called Appleyard lived there at the time of the Civil War, and were fervent supporters of the Royalist cause. After giving shelter to some fugitive Royalists escaping from Sandal Castle in 1644, the lady of the house was arrested and subsequently tried and beheaded. Her spirit was said to walk in Church Lane on the nights of full moons, carrying her head beneath her arm. The story probably says a great deal about the state of mind of its perpetrators and little of historical value. Alongside Church Lane today, between the Hall and the Church, stand a number of ancient yew trees, reputedly planted in the thirteenth century to provide wood for bows.

The Cherry Tree Inn, a popular haunt, stands on or near to the site of a medieval hostelry which has borne different names at different times. In the eighteenth century it was known as the Cherry Tree – perhaps derived from a cherry orchard behind it. By 1830 it was referred to as the Shoulder of Mutton, in 1870 as The Globe, and in recent times it has reverted to its original name. Here, from the mid-seventeenth century, the Overseers of the Poor of the parish met to allocate poor relief. Here also the churchwardens met each Easter to settle accounts and to elect the parish constable and highway surveyor; and here in 1816 some of the leading gentlemen in the district met to establish a school for 'the children of the lower orders' who were said to be

In 1816 leading citizens in the High Hoyland district agreed to establish a school within the parish. It was decided that it should be sited between High Hoyland and Clayton West, so that it could serve both communities. Located at the top of Hollinghouse Lane, this building is now also a private residence.

'destitute of the means of a useful education'. That school (to be built between High Hoyland and Clayton West so that it could serve both communities) was housed in a building, now a private residence, near to Winterhill Farm.

Haigh

THE SMALL COMMUNITY AT HAIGH has probably experienced more changes during the past eighty years than any other community in the valley. Gone is most of the former turnpike road from Barnsley to Grange Moor, carried over delightful stone bridges in a gentler age. A small stretch can just be seen outside Mill Farm, and one of the toll cottages survives though incorporated into a modern house and hardly recognisable. Now the village is starkly intersected by the Ml motorway with one of its exits and associated roundabout. Gone also is the Swithen bleach works, which closed in 1922 leaving a small reservoir on the east side of the motorway as the only reminder of what was, in the mid-nineteenth century, a thriving concern. The village was once heavily dependent on coal mining, but the former colliery closed in the 1960s, the brick terraced houses in Haigh Lane having been built to house some its employees. Near to the colliery was the railway

Bretton Mill New Bar. Standing on the boundary between Haigh and West Bretton, it was built as a tollkeeper's cottage on the Barnsley-Grange Moor turnpike. It has been incorporated into a modern house.

The former Haigh Station. It was closed during what came to be known as the 'Beeching era' and demolished in the 1960s.

station which was once used by villagers from Haigh and West Bretton, as well as by the Allendale family of Bretton Hall when travelling to London or to their Northumberland estates. That became a casualty of the 'Beeching Era.' Gone also is the former Methodist New Connexion chapel which stood directly on the route of the motorway and which was replaced by a modern brick structure in Haigh Lane; and the post office which, in 1988, was converted into a public house.

What does remain is the delightful Hall, formerly the residence of members of the Cotton family. The Cottons were actively involved in the local iron industry. In the seventeenth century William Cotton moved from Cheshire to the South Yorkshire village of Wortley. From there he moved to Silkstone and later to Denby, where he died in 1675. From about that time his descendants became settled at what was called 'The Hague'. The house can be traced back in written sources to Tudor times, but it was substantially modified in the eighteenth century. By 1720 the Cottons had become very involved with the nearby Bretton Furnace and were increasingly linked with the Spencers of Cawthorne through various agreements and partnerships. With the demise of the iron industry they came into straitened circumstances and, in 1793, sold their Haigh Estate to Lt Col Thomas Richard Beaumont, of Bretton Hall, for £19,800.

Although the station has gone, the railway has not. It was built under an Act of Parliament of 1845 as part of the 'Sheffield, Rotherham, Barnsley, Wakefield, Huddersfield and Goole' line, later to be absorbed by the Lancashire and Yorkshire Railway Company. Its main purpose was the transportation of coal from the district to the port of Goole. At the time it was built, the first flush of what has been called 'railway mania' was dying down, and what had been planned as a double track was reduced to a single line passing through the 1.59 km Woolley Edge tunnel. The line was opened in 1850 and soon turned out to be inadequate for the volume of traffic upon it. A second line was built in 1855 but the single tunnel remained and became a bottleneck until 1902, when a second tunnel was bored. Large heaps of the excavated shale can still be seen, piled on the east side of the motorway, now somewhat disguised by considerable vegetation.

Rising above the village, on its eastern side, is Woolley Edge, a prominent landmark which once served as a beacon station. The last time it was fired in a time of national emergency appears to have been in 1805, the era of Napoleon, when the possibility of an invasion troubled many people. On August 15th of that year, the beacon was lit after it was thought that a similar beacon had been lit at Pontefract.

Haigh Hall. Occupying a site that appears to have been inhabited since at least the sixteenth century, it was substantially remodelled for the Cotton family in the eighteenth century.

This was the signal to summon the Staincross Volunteers – the Home Guard of the time! It took some fourteen hours for some 600 men to assemble. Many had to walk up to 12 miles to hear their Commanding Officer, Walter Spencer-Stanhope of Cannon Hall. It was probably little consolation to them to discover that it was a false alarm. The Pontefract Beacon had not been lit. The people in Woolley had been misled by the firing of a nearby brick kiln.

Woolley Edge Bonfire commemorating the Coronation of King Edward VII in 1902 (Height 42ft.; weight 135 tons; circumference at base 35 yds.; paraffin 80 gallons; gas tar 300 gallons.)

The former Haigh Methodist Chapel

Several of the delightful aspects of Haigh were wiped out when the M1 motorway was constructed. This was the point at which Jebb Lane from High Hoyland joined the former Barnsley–Grange Moor turnpike. The cottages remain, but the bridges do not.

Bibliography

Addy, J., *A Coal and Iron Community in the Industrial Revolution*, London, Longman, 1969

Addy, J. (ed), *A Further History of Penistone*, Penistone, 1965

Addy, J. (ed), *A History of the Denby Dale Urban District Council*, Denby Dale, 1974

Ahier, P., *The Legends and Traditions of Huddersfield and its District,* Huddersfield, 1941

Andrews, C.R., *The Story of Wortley Ironworks*, 3rd edition, Nottingham, R. Milward Ltd., 1975

Arnold, T.P., *Methodism in a West Yorkshire Village*, Denby Dale Methodist Church, 1999

Baines, E., *History, Directory and Gazetteer of the County of York*, Leeds, 1822

Bairstow, M., *The Huddersfield and Sheffield Junction Railway*, Halifax, 1993

Banks, W.S., *Walks about Wakefield*, 2nd edition, Wakefield, Wakefield Historical Publications, 1983

Barber, B.J., and Beresford, M.W., *The West Riding County Council 1889-1974*, Wakefield, 1979

Bielby, A.R., *Churches and Chapels of Kirklees*, Kirklees Library and Museum Service, 1978

Brownhill, R.N., *The Penistone Scene*, Penistone, Bridge Publications, 1987

Buck, S., *Yorkshire Sketchbook*, Wakefield, Reproduced from the Lansdowne Ms. 914 in the British Library by Wakefield Historical Publications, 1979

Caffyn, L., *Workers' Housing in West Yorkshire 1750-1920*, Her Majesty's Stationery Office, 1986

Carpenter, E., *Cantuar: The Archbishops in their Office*, London, Mowbray, 1988

Carter, R.A., *A Visitors' Guide to Yorkshire Churches*, Bradford, Watmoughs, 1976

Dale, B., *Yorkshire Puritanism and Early Nonconformity*, Bradford, 1906

Dransfield, J.N., *A History of the Parish of Penistone*, Penistone, 1906

Elton, A. and Foster, E., *Yorkshire Piety and Persuasion*, University of Leeds School of Education, 1985

Fairholm, P.H., *Cawthorne Boundary Walk*, Cawthorne, 1986
Falconer, K., *Guide to England's Industrial Heritage*, London, Batsford, 1980
Flack, H. and Wainwright, T., *A Short Survey of the History of the Clayton West Methodist Circuit*, Skelmanthorpe, 1959

Giles, C., *Rural Houses of West Yorkshire*, Her Majesty's Stationery Office, 1986
Gilks, J.A., *A Neolithic Occupation Site at Castle Hill, Denby, near Huddersfield, Yorkshire*, Wakefield, West Yorkshire Metropolitan County Council Archeological Research Committee, 1974
Goodchild, J., *Caphouse Colliery and the Denby Grange Collieries,* Wakefield, Wakefield Historical Publications, 1983

Haigh, E.A.H. (ed.), *Huddersfield – a Most Handsome Town*, Kirklees Cultural Services, 1992
Hayes, G., *Stationary Steam Engines*, Princes Risborough, Shire Publications, 1995
Heath, C., *Deneby: Farmstead of the Danes*, Huddersfield, Richard Netherwood Ltd., 1997
Heath, C., *The History of the Denby Dale Pies*, Denby Dale, J.R. Nicolls, 1998
Hey, D., *Yorkshire from AD 1000*, London, Longman, 1986
Hey, D., *Family History and Local History in England*, London, Longman, 1987
Holmes, D.H., *The Mining and Quarrying Industries in the Huddersfield District*, Huddersfield, Tolson Memorial Museum, 1967
Hoskins, W.G., *Fieldwork in Local History*, London, Faber, 1967
Hunter, J., *The History and Topography of South Yorkshire*, London, 1831
Hunter, J., *The Rise of the Old Dissent exemplified in the Life of Oliver Heywood*, London, 1842

Jackson, G.B., *All Saints' Church, Cawthorne 1880-1980*, Cawthorne, 1980
Jackson, G.B., *Cawthorne 1790-1990*, Cawthorne, Cawthorne Victoria Jubilee Museum, 1991

Lawton, F., *Historical Notes of Skelmanthorpe and District*, Place and date of publication uncertain

Macdonald, Alice, *The Fortunes of a Family*, Edinburgh, T. & A. Constable, 1928

Mallinson, J., *History of Methodism in Huddersfield, Holmfirth and Denby Dale*, London, Charles H. Kelly, 1898

Marshall, J., *The Lancashire and Yorkshire Railway*, Newton Abbott, David & Charles, 1969

Mee, A., *Yorkshire - West Riding*, London, Hodder and Stoughton, 1950

Morris, R.W., *Yorkshire through Place Names*, Newton Abbot, David and Charles, 1982

Parker, G.F., *A Description of Emley*, Emley, Date uncertain

Pevsner, N., *The Buildings of England: Yorkshire – the West Riding*, London, Penguin Books, 1959

Pobjoy, N.H., *A History of Emley – a West Riding Village*, Driffield, The Ridings Publishing Company, 1970

Pratt, C.T., *A History of Cawthorne*, Cawthorne, 1882

Prince, J.T., *The History and Topography of the Parish of Silkstone*, Penistone, 1922

Raistrick, A., *Industrial Archaeology*, London, Granada Publishing, 1973

Rennie, Broun and Shirreff, *General View of the Agriculture of the West Riding of Yorkshire*, London, 1774

Richardson, J., *The Local Historian's Encyclopedia*, New Barnet, Historical Publications Ltd, 1977

Rogers, A., *Approaches to Local History*, London, Longman, 1977

Senior, J., *The Last of the Day-Hole Miners*, Darley Dale, Walk and Write Ltd., 1997

Sheeran, G., *Landscape Gardens in West Yorkshire 1680-1880*, Wakefield, 1990

South and West Yorkshire Federation of Women's Institutes, *The South and West Yorkshire Village Book,* Newbury, Countryside Books, 1991

Smith, A.H., *The Place Names of the West Riding of Yorkshire*, Cambridge, C.U.P., 1961

Smith, D.J., *Aspects of Life in Old Cawthorne*, Sheffield,1988

Tarbatt, A., *Camp of the Cumbrians*, Cumberworth, 1983

Taylor, H., *The Coward Family and the Bleachworks at Swithen*, article in 'Old West Riding', Vol. 12, 1992

Thompson, E.P., *The Making of the English Working Class*, London, Penguin, 1963

Thornes, R.C.N., *West Yorkshire – 'A Noble Scene of Industry'*, Wakefield, 1981

Thorpe, J. and T., *Emley and its Past – being extracts from the Almanack compiled in 1884 by the late John and Thomas Thorpe*, Emley, 1936

Turner, J. Horsfall, *The Rev. Oliver Heywood BA, 1630-1702*, Brighouse, 1832

Umpleby, T., *Water Mills and Furnaces on the Yorkshire Dearne and its Tributaries*, Wakefield, Wakefield Historical Publications, 2000

Wainwright, T., *Our Methodist Heritage*, Skelmanthorpe, 1986
Wilkinson, J.F., *Farmstead of the Britons – the Story of a West Riding Village*, Penistone, Bridge Publications, 1989
Wright, S.J., *Bretton, The Beaumonts and a Bureaucracy*, Wakefield, Wakefield Historical Publications, 2001

Yorkshire Archaeological Journal, *The Poll Tax Returns for the West Riding of Yorkshire – 1379*, Leeds, 1882
Yorkshire Archaeological Record Series:
Vol. XVI: *Yorkshire Lay Subsidies*, Leeds, 1894
Vol. LXIX: *Yorkshire Deeds*, Leeds, 1931
Vol. LXXVI: *Yorkshire Deeds*, Leeds, 1972
Young, K., *Chapel*, London, Eyre-Methuen, 1972

The Denby Dale Parish Countryside Project has published Village Trails for Clayton West, Denby Dale and Skelmanthorpe – copies of which may be obtained locally – and West Bretton Parish Council has published a guide to the footpaths in that vicinity which contains substantial historical information about the village.

Index